2A

# Math in Focus®
## Singapore Math®
by Marshall Cavendish

# Extra Practice

**Author**
Meena Newaskar

**Marshall Cavendish**
Education

U.S. Distributor

Houghton
Mifflin
Harcourt

© 2015 Marshall Cavendish Education Pte Ltd

**Published by Marshall Cavendish Education**
*An imprint of Marshall Cavendish Education Pte Ltd*
Times Centre, 1 New Industrial Road, Singapore 536196
Customer Service Hotline: (65) 6213 9444
US Office Tel: (1-914) 332 8888  Fax: (1-914) 332 8882
E-mail: tmesales@mceducation.com
Website: www.mceducation.com

Distributed by
**Houghton Mifflin Harcourt**
222 Berkeley Street
Boston, MA 02116
Tel: 617-351-5000
Website: www.hmheducation.com/mathinfocus

First published 2015

*Math in Focus*® Extra Practice 2A
ISBN 978-0-544-19402-1

Printed in Singapore

2  3  4  5  6  7  8     1401     20  19  18  17  16  15
4500495929                       A B C D E

# Contents

# Introducing

# Math in Focus®

## Extra Practice

*Extra Practice 2A* and *2B*, written to complement *Math in Focus®: Singapore Math®* by Marshall Cavendish Grade 2, offer further practice very similar to the Practice exercises in the Student Books and Workbooks for on-level students.

*Extra Practice* provides ample questions to reinforce all the concepts taught, and includes challenging questions in the Put on Your Thinking Cap! pages. These pages provide extra nonroutine problem-solving opportunities, strengthening critical thinking skills.

*Extra Practice* is an excellent option for homework, or may be used in class or after school. It is intended for students who simply need more practice to become confident, or secure students who are aiming for excellence.

 **Numbers to 1,000**

## Lesson 1   Counting

Write the numbers shown by the base-ten blocks.

**1.**

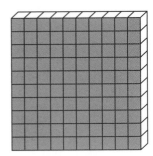

_____

**2.**

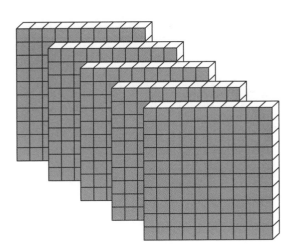

_____

**3.**

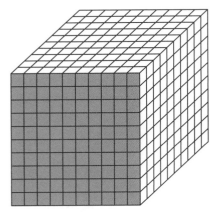

_____

**Write the numbers shown by the base-ten blocks.**
**Then write the numbers in words.**

4.

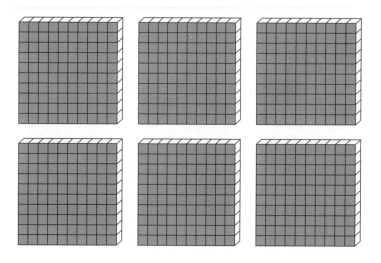

_____

_____

5.

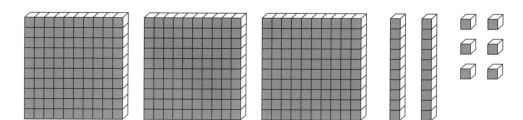

_____

_____

6.

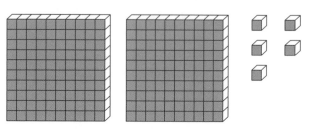

_____

_____

Name: _____ Date: _____

● **Write the numbers in words.**

7. ⟨ 324 ⟩ _____

8. ⟨ 592 ⟩ _____

9. ⟨ 748 ⟩ _____

10. ⟨ 416 ⟩ _____

● 11. ⟨ 209 ⟩ _____

**Write the numbers.**

12. Four hundred fifteen _____

13. Eight hundred ninety-eight _____

14. One hundred forty-two _____

15. Two hundred six _____

16. One thousand _____

## Find the missing numbers.

+1     +1

**17.**     325, 326, 327, _____, _____, _____

**18.**     432, 433, 434, _____, _____, _____

**19.**     201, 202, 203, _____, _____, _____

+10   +10

**20.**     280, 290, _____, _____, _____, 330

**21.**     315, 325, 335, _____, _____, _____

**22.**     461, 471, 481, _____, _____, _____

+100 +100

**23.**     210, 310, 410, _____, _____, _____

**24.**     306, 406, 506, _____, _____, _____

**25.**     119, 219, 319, _____, _____, _____

# Lesson 2   Place Value

**Look at the place-value charts.**
**Then write the numbers in standard form.**

1.

| Hundreds | Tens | Ones |
|---|---|---|
| | | |
| | | |
| | | |

2.

| Hundreds | Tens | Ones |
|---|---|---|
| | | |
| | | |
| | | |

## Look at the place-value chart.
## Then write the number in standard form.

3.

| Hundreds | Tens | Ones |
|---|---|---|
| | | |
| | | |

## Fill in the place-value chart.

4.

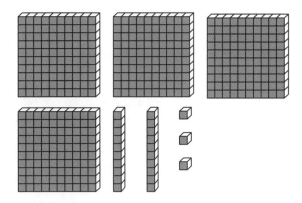

| Hundreds | Tens | Ones |
|---|---|---|
| | | |

5.

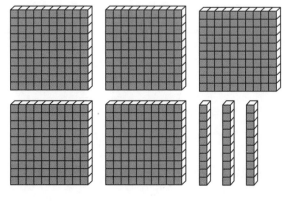

| Hundreds | Tens | Ones |
|---|---|---|
| | | |

**6.**

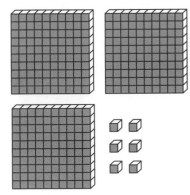

| Hundreds | Tens | Ones |
|----------|------|------|
|          |      |      |

## Fill in the blanks.

**7.**

834

  **a.** The digit _____ is in the ones place.

  **b.** The digit _____ is in the tens place.

  **c.** The digit _____ is in the hundreds place.

**8.**

710

  **a.** The digit _____ is in the ones place.

  **b.** The digit _____ is in the tens place.

  **c.** The digit _____ is in the hundreds place.

**Fill in the blanks.**

9.

925

    **a.**   The digit _____ is in the ones place.

    **b.**   The digit _____ is in the tens place.

    **c.**   The digit _____ is in the hundreds place

10.   Write the greatest possible three-digit number using the digits
       0, 4, and 7.

| Hundreds | Tens | Ones |
|----------|------|------|
|          |      |      |

11.   Write the greatest possible three-digit number using the digits
       1, 3, and 6.

| Hundreds | Tens | Ones |
|----------|------|------|
|          |      |      |

● **Look at each number on the fish.**
**Then write the missing numbers and words.**

12.
= _____ + 70 + 5

= _____ hundreds + 7 tens + 5 ones

Write the number in word form.

_____

13.
= 800 + _____ + 6

= _____ hundreds + _____ tens + 6 ones

Write the number in word form.

_____

**Write the missing numbers.**

14.     739 = 700 + 30 + _____

15.     624 = _____ + 20 + 4

16.     908 = 900 + _____ + 8

17.     264 = 200 + _____ + 4

**Write the missing numbers.**

**18.**   700 + 80 + 2 = _____

**19.**   300 + 4 = _____

**20.**   500 + 30 + 6 = _____

**21.**   200 + 90 = _____

**Write the missing numbers.**

**22.**   5 hundreds 2 tens 1 one = _____ + _____ + _____

**23.**   2 hundreds 6 tens 0 ones = _____ + _____ + _____

**24.**   The value of 7 in 678 is _____.

**25.**   The value of 5 in 536 is _____.

**26.**   470 = 4 hundreds _____ tens 0 ones

**27.**   848 = 8 hundreds _____ tens 8 ones

# Lesson 3   Comparing Numbers

**Check (✔) the correct sentences.**

**1.**

630 is less than 603. ☐

603 is less than 630. ☐

603 is greater than 630. ☐

630 is greater than 603. ☐

**2.**

832 is less than 823. ☐

832 is greater than 823. ☐

823 is less than 832. ☐

823 is greater than 832. ☐

## Check (✔) the correct sentences.

**3.**    472 is less than 492.

431 is less than 389.

399 is greater than 395.

745 is greater than 7 hundreds and 5 ones.

## Compare.
## Circle the correct answer.

**4.**    Which number is greater?

**5.**    Which number is less?

**6.**    Which number is greater?

**7.** Which number is less?

680    638

**Write _greater than_ or _less than_ in the blanks.**

**8.** 471 is _____ 106.

**9.** 823 is _____ 833.

**10.** 587 is _____ 692.

**11.** 319 is _____ 103.

**Compare.**
**Write > or < in the**  **.**

**12.** 510 ◯ 501

**13.** 909 ◯ 990

**14.** 453 ◯ 389

> means greater than.
< means less than.

**Compare.**
**Write > or < in the ◯.**

**15.** 300 ◯ 299

**16.** 888 ◯ 1000

**17.** 760 ◯ 607

**Write *T* for true or *F* for false.**

**18.** 60 is greater than 600.

**19.** 746 is less than 1,000.

**20.** 310 is less than 301.

**21.** 944 is greater than 499.

**22.** 682 < 628

**23.** 131 > 113

# Lesson 4   Order and Pattern

**Order the numbers.**
**Use the place-value chart to help you.**

**1.**

|  | Hundreds | Tens | Ones |
|---|---|---|---|
| 439 | 4 | 3 | 9 |
| 254 | 2 | 5 | 4 |
| 617 | 6 | 1 | 7 |
| 381 | 3 | 8 | 1 |

_____, _____, _____, _____
      least

**2.**

|  | Hundreds | Tens | Ones |
|---|---|---|---|
| 431 | 4 | 3 | 1 |
| 314 | 3 | 1 | 4 |
| 134 | 1 | 3 | 4 |
| 413 | 4 | 1 | 3 |

_____, _____, _____, _____
      greatest

**Name:** _____  **Date:** _____

## Order the numbers from least to greatest.

**3.**

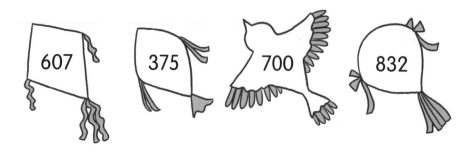

_____, _____, _____, _____
least

## Order the numbers from greatest to least.

**4.**

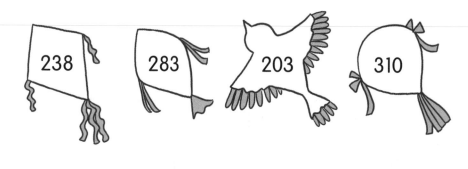

_____, _____, _____, _____
greatest

## Make four different sets of three-digit numbers.
## Order them from least to greatest.

**5.**

_____, _____, _____, _____
least

## What is the missing number?

**6.**

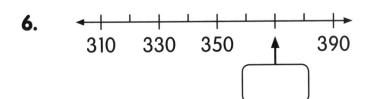

**7.**

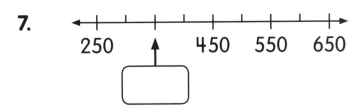

## Fill in the missing numbers.

**8.**

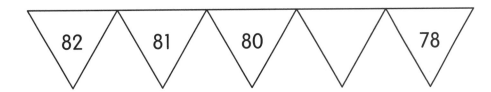

82   81   80      78

**9.**

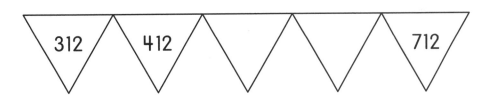

312   412         712

**10.**

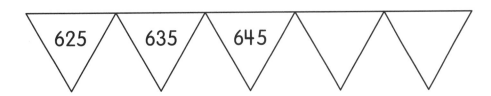

625   635   645

**11.**

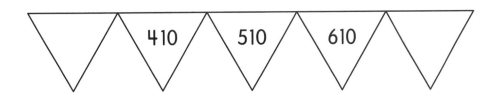

410   510   610

 Put on Your Thinking Cap!

**Fill in the blanks.**

 +  +  = $30

 +  = $20

 +  = $18

 = _____

 +  = _____

 +  +  = _____

# CHAPTER 2 Addition up to 1,000

## Lesson 1 Addition and Subtraction Facts Within 20

**Fill in the missing numbers.**
**Add mentally.**

1.  7 + 5 = ?
    7 + <u>3</u> = 10
    <u>10</u> + 2 = <u>12</u>
    So, 7 + 5 = _____

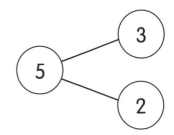

2.  6 + 9 = ?

    6 + _____ = _____

    _____ + _____ = _____

    So, 6 + 9 = _____

3.  5 + 8 = _____

4.  8 + 6 = _____

5.  7 + 6 = _____

6.  9 + 5 = _____

7.  8 + 7 = _____

8.  7 + 9 = _____

9.  9 + 9 = _____

Name: _____     Date: _____

**Fill in the missing numbers.**
**Subtract mentally.**

10.    12 – 6 = ?
       10 – <u>6</u> = 4
       <u>4</u> + 2 = 6
       So, 12 – 6 = _____

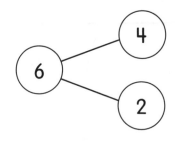

11.    13 – 8 = ?

       10 – _____ = _____

       _____ + _____ = _____

       So, 13 – 8 = _____

12.    12 – 9 = _____       13.   15 – 7 = _____

14.    11 – 6 = _____       15.   14 – 9 = _____

16.    13 – 7 = _____       17.   16 – 9 = _____

18.    17 – 8 = _____

# Lesson 2  Addition Without Regrouping

**Add.**

1.  643 + 222 = ?

    Add the ones.

    3 ones + 2 ones = _____ ones

    $$\begin{array}{r} 6 \quad 4 \quad 3 \\ + \ 2 \quad 2 \quad 2 \\ \hline \end{array}$$

    Add the tens.

    4 tens + 2 tens = _____ tens

    Add the hundreds.

    6 hundreds + 2 hundreds = _____ hundreds

    643 + 222 = _____

2.  $$\begin{array}{r} 3 \quad 4 \quad 1 \\ + \ 5 \quad 2 \quad 7 \\ \hline \end{array}$$

3.  $$\begin{array}{r} 1 \quad 7 \quad 4 \\ + \ 4 \quad 2 \quad 5 \\ \hline \end{array}$$

4.  761 + 108 = _____

    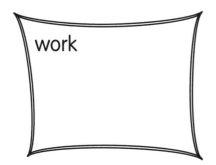

    work

5.  273 + 516 = _____

    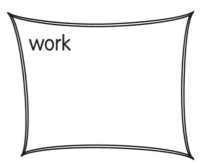

    work

**Solve.**

6.  Pia scores 128 points in a computer game.
    Jahara scores 311 points in the same computer game.
    How many points do they score in all?

    They score _____ points in all.

7.  Mrs. Jones bakes 150 snacks for a bake sale.
    Mr. Lim bakes 110 snacks for the bake sale.
    How many snacks do they bake in all?

    They bake _____ snacks in all.

# Lesson 3   Addition with Regrouping in Ones

**Add and regroup the ones.**

1.   549 + 425 = ?

Add and regroup the ones.

9 ones + 5 ones = _____ ones

= _____ ten _____ ones

$$\begin{array}{r} 5\ \ 4\ \ 9 \\ +\ \ 4\ \ 2\ \ 5 \\ \hline \end{array}$$

Add the tens.

1 ten + 4 tens + 2 tens = _____ tens

Add the hundreds.

5 hundreds + 4 hundreds = _____ hundreds

549 + 425 = _____

2.   $$\begin{array}{r} 4\ \ 5\ \ 7 \\ +\ \ 2\ \ 3\ \ 4 \\ \hline \end{array}$$

3.   $$\begin{array}{r} 1\ \ 5\ \ 8 \\ +\ \ 3\ \ 1\ \ 2 \\ \hline \end{array}$$

4.   114 + 127 = _____

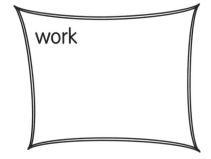

work

5.   729 + 103 = _____

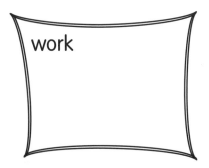

work

**Solve.**

6.    John and Cameron bowl on the same team.
      John scores 124 points.
      Cameron scores 136 points.
      How many points do they score in all?

      James and Cameron score _____ points in all.

7.    A book sale lasts for two days.
      On the first day, 348 books are sold.
      On the second day, 239 books are sold.
      How many books are sold during the two day sale?

      _____ books are sold during the two day sale.

# Lesson 4   Addition with Regrouping in Tens

## Add and regroup the tens.

**1.**   293 + 465 = ?

Add the ones.

3 ones + 5 ones = _____ ones

$$\begin{array}{r} 2\ 9\ 3 \\ +\ 4\ 6\ 5 \\ \hline \end{array}$$

Add and regroup the tens.

9 tens + 6 tens = _____ tens

= _____ hundred _____ tens

Add the hundreds.

1 hundred + 2 hundreds + 4 hundreds = _____ hundreds

293 + 465 = _____

**2.**
$$\begin{array}{r} 3\ 7\ 2 \\ +\ 1\ 4\ 4 \\ \hline \end{array}$$

**3.**
$$\begin{array}{r} 6\ 5\ 4 \\ +\ 2\ 7\ 3 \\ \hline \end{array}$$

**4.**   151 + 474 = _____

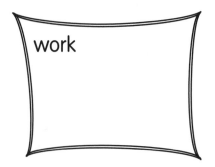
work

**5.**   778 + 191 = _____

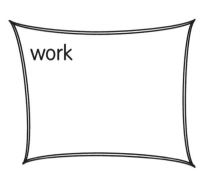
work

**Solve.**

6.  A farmer sold 385 eggs.
    She has 74 eggs left.
    How many eggs did she have at first?

    She had _____ eggs at first.

7.  Andy had 546 stamps.
    His brother Ryan gave him 273 stamps.
    How many stamps does Andy have now?

    Andy has _____ stamps now.

# Lesson 5 Addition with Regrouping in Ones and Tens

**Add.**

| 1. | T |
|---|---|
| $$\begin{array}{r} 1\ 5\ 8 \\ +\quad 8\ 9 \\ \hline \end{array}$$ | |

| 2. | E |
|---|---|
| $$\begin{array}{r} 2\ 5\ 5 \\ +\ 1\ 7\ 6 \\ \hline \end{array}$$ | |

| 3. | M |
|---|---|
| $$\begin{array}{r} 1\ 4\ 6 \\ +\ 2\ 6\ 6 \\ \hline \end{array}$$ | |

| 4. | R |
|---|---|
| $$\begin{array}{r} 1\ 9\ 7 \\ +\ 3\ 7\ 8 \\ \hline \end{array}$$ | |

| 5. | S |
|---|---|
| $$\begin{array}{r} 5\ 7\ 3 \\ +\ 2\ 4\ 9 \\ \hline \end{array}$$ | |

| 6. | A |
|---|---|
| $$\begin{array}{r} 4\ 7\ 5 \\ +\ 3\ 6\ 9 \\ \hline \end{array}$$ | |

Write the letters that match the numbers.
What word do you spell?

_____ _____ _____ _____ _____ _____ your Math!
412   844   822   247   431   575

**Solve.**

7.    Mia has 248 stickers.
      Philip has 94 stickers more than Mia has.
      How many stickers does Philip have?

Philip has _____ stickers.

8.    Michael solves 209 math problems.
      Joshua solves 85 more problems than Michael solves.
      How many problems does Joshua solve in all?

Joshua solves _____ problems in all.

# Put on Your Thinking Cap!

1. Use the numbers below to fill in the boxes.
   You can use each number only once.

## 1 2 4 5 6 9

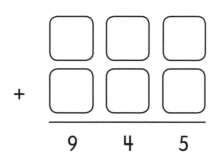

**2.**   Make two 3-digit numbers from these numbers.
        Use each number only once.
        What are the two 3-digit numbers that give the least
        answer when you add them?

$$7 \quad 4 \quad 2 \quad 6 \quad 1 \quad 5$$

 CHAPTER **3** # Subtraction up to 1,000

## Lesson 1   Subtraction Without Regrouping

**Subtract.**

**1.**  543 – 132 = ?

Subtract the ones.

3 ones – 2 ones = _____ one

Subtract the tens.

4 tens – 3 tens = _____ ten

Subtract the hundreds.

5 hundreds – 1 hundred = _____ hundreds

543 – 132 = _____

```
    5  4  3
 -  1  3  2
 _____
```

**Check.**  ( _____ )

```
 +  1  3  2
 _____
    5  4  3
```

**2.**
```
    6  9  6
 -  1  8  2
 _____
```

**3.**
```
    8  9  6
 -  5  7  3
 _____
```

**4.**  783 – 671 = _____

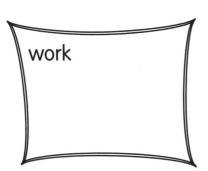
work

**5.**  476 – 324 = _____

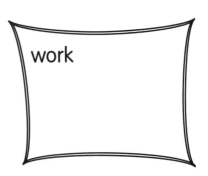
work

**Solve.**

6.     Ling has 498 beads.
       She uses 254 beads to make a necklace.
       How many beads does Ling have left?

       Ling has _____ beads left.

7.     Mr. Garcia drives 282 miles on Saturday.
       Mr. Garcia drives 110 miles less on Sunday than
       he did on Saturday.
       How many miles does Mr. Garcia drive on Sunday?

       Mr. Garcia drives _____ miles on Sunday.

# Lesson 2 Subtraction with Regrouping in Tens and Ones

**Regroup the tens and ones.**
**Then subtract.**

**1.** 843 − 425 = ?

843 − 425

= 8 hundreds 4 tens 3 ones
  − 4 hundreds 2 tens 5 ones

= 8 hundreds 3 tens _____ ones
  − 4 hundreds 2 tens 5 ones

= 4 hundreds _____ tens _____ ones

= _____

843 − 425 = _____

```
    8  4  3
 −  4  2  5
_____
```

**Check.**

```
    (          )
 +  4  2  5
_____
    8  4  3
```

**2.**
```
    8  9  6
 −  2  5  8
_____
```

**3.**
```
    7  5  8
 −  5  2  9
_____
```

**4.** 321 − 108 = _____

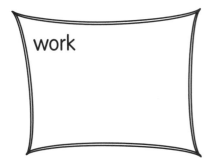
work

**5.** 647 − 429 = _____

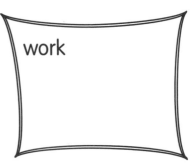
work

**Solve.**

6.    Jacob has 394 coins in his coin collection.
      He gives 88 coins to George.
      How many coins does Jacob have now?




      Jacob has _____ coins now.

7.    455 children visit the museum on Friday.
      129 more children visit the museum on Friday than on Thursday.
      How many children visit the museum on Thursday?




      _____ children visit the museum on Thursday.

# Lesson 3  Subtraction with Regrouping in Hundreds and Tens

**Regroup the hundreds and tens.**
**Then subtract.**

**1.**    752 – 170 = ?

752 – 170

= 7 hundreds 5 tens 2 ones
  – 1 hundred 7 tens

= 6 hundreds _____ tens 2 ones – 1 hundred 7 tens

= _____ hundreds _____ tens _____ ones

= _____

752 – 170 = _____

```
   7  5  2
-  1  7  0
_____
```

**Check.**  ⬭

```
+  1  7  0
_____
   7  5  2
```

**2.**
```
   6  4  7
-  4  6  2
_____
```

**3.**
```
   8  7  6
-  2  9  5
_____
```

**4.**    939 – 587 = _____

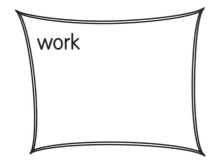
work

**5.**    549 – 372 = _____

work

**Solve.**

6.  Matthew has 345 baseball cards.
    David has 172 baseball cards.
    How many more cards does Matthew have than David?

    Matthew has _____ more cards than David.

7.  A tea set costs $182.
    A dinner set costs $258.
    How much less does the tea set cost than the dinner set?

    The tea set costs $_____ less than the dinner set.

Name: _____  Date: _____

# Lesson 4  Subtraction with Regrouping in Hundreds, Tens, and Ones

**Regroup.
Then subtract.**

1.  461 – 179 = ?

    461 – 179

    = 4 hundreds 6 tens 1 one

      – 1 hundred 7 tens 9 ones

$$
\begin{array}{r}
4\ \ 6\ \ 1 \\
-\ 1\ \ 7\ \ 9 \\
\hline
\end{array}
$$

    = 3 hundreds _____ tens 11 ones – 1 hundred 7 tens 9 ones

    = _____ hundreds _____ tens _____ ones

    = _____

    461 – 179 = _____

    **Check.** ⬭

$$
\begin{array}{r}
+\ 1\ \ 7\ \ 9 \\
\hline
4\ \ 6\ \ 1
\end{array}
$$

2.
$$
\begin{array}{r}
4\ \ 3\ \ 5 \\
-\ 1\ \ 7\ \ 6 \\
\hline
\end{array}
$$

3.
$$
\begin{array}{r}
6\ \ 1\ \ 4 \\
-\ 2\ \ 6\ \ 7 \\
\hline
\end{array}
$$

4.  571 – 108 = _____

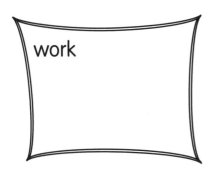

work

5.  735 – 257 = _____

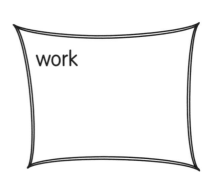

work

## Solve.

6.  Lara makes 430 glasses of juice for a school fair.
    She makes 145 glasses of apple juice.
    The rest are glasses of orange juice.
    How many glasses of orange juice does Lara make?

    Lara makes _____ glasses of orange juice.

7.  Emily has 245 books in her library.
    She gives 187 books to her cousin.
    How many books are left in Emily's library?

    There are _____ books left in Emily's library.

# Lesson 5   Subtraction Across Zeros

**Regroup.**
**Then subtract.**

**1.**   400 – 283 = ?

```
  4 0 0
– 2 8 3
_____
```

400 = 4 hundreds

= 3 hundreds _____ tens

= 3 hundreds _____ tens _____ ones

400 – 283 = _____

**Check.**

```
      ⌈‾‾‾‾‾⌉
+ 2 8 3
_____
  4 0 0
```

**2.**
```
  5 0 0
– 3 4 6
_____
```

**3.**
```
  3 0 0
– 1 7 6
_____
```

**4.**
```
  6 0 0
– 1 9 5
_____
```

**5.**
```
  7 0 0
– 3 6 5
_____
```

**6.**   800 – 348 = _____

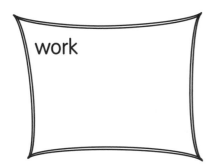

work

**7.**   900 – 609 = _____

work

**Solve.**

8.      A farmer has 400 apples and 378 oranges.
        How many more apples than oranges does he have?

        He has _____ more apples than oranges.

9.      There are 800 men at a soccer match.
        There are 168 fewer women than men.
        How many women are there at the soccer match?

        There are _____ women at the soccer match.

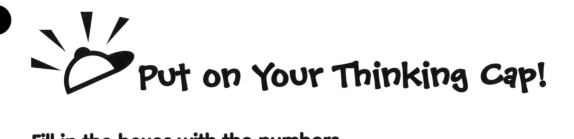

# Put on Your Thinking Cap!

**Fill in the boxes with the numbers.**
**Use each number only once.**

1.    **11   8   13   9   14   10   12**

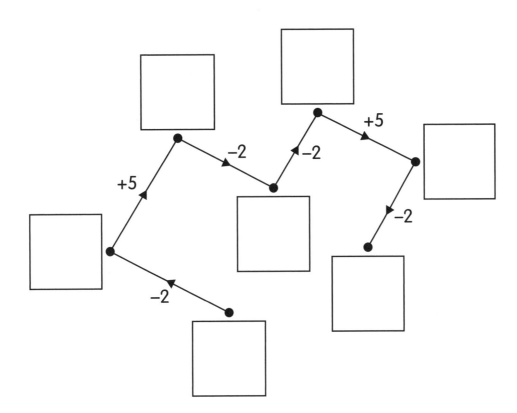

**2.** Kylie has 4 coin banks filled with coins.
The number of coins in each bank is shown.

Bank A        Bank B        Bank C        Bank D

Which three coin banks have 740 coins in all?

Bank _____, Bank _____, and Bank _____
contain 740 coins in all.

# CHAPTER 4 Using Bar Models: Addition and Subtraction

## Lesson 1  Using Part-Part-Whole in Addition and Subtraction

**Solve.**
**Use the bar models to help you.**

1.  There are 28 boys and 19 girls in a class.
    How many students are there in all?

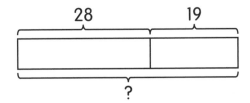

    There are _____ students in all.

2.  Mrs. Marie gives $154 to Chantel.
    She gives $78 to David.
    How much money does Mrs. Marie give in all?

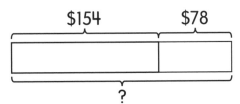

    Mrs. Marie gives $_____ in all.

**Solve.**
**Draw bar models to help you.**

3.  Mrs. Diaz buys 21 balloons for a birthday party.
    On the way home, 3 balloons burst.
    How many balloons does Mrs. Diaz have now?

    Mrs. Diaz has _____ balloons now.

4.  Jamie has 500 red beads and blue beads in all.
    She has 238 red beads.
    How many blue beads does Jamie have?

    Jamie has _____ blue beads.

# Lesson 2  Adding On and Taking Away Sets

**Solve.**
**Use the bar models to help you.**

**1.** Ella has 145 marbles.
Her mother gives her 37 more.
How many marbles does Ella have in all?

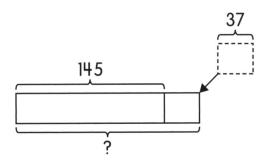

Ella has _____ marbles in all.

**2.** The school hall has 253 chairs in it.
129 new chairs are added to the hall.
How many chairs are there in all?

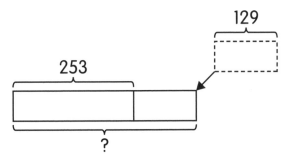

There are _____ chairs in all.

**Solve.**
**Use the bar models to help you.**

**3.** Leena has 178 crayons.
Leena gives her sister some and has 25 crayons left.
How many crayons did Leena give her sister?

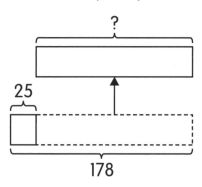

Leena gave her sister _____ crayons.

**4.** A baker has 206 muffins.
He sells 143 muffins.
How many muffins does the baker have left?

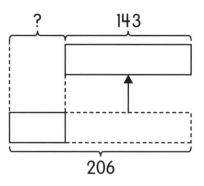

The baker has _____ muffins left.

**Solve.**
**Draw bar models to help you.**

5.  Pedro has 48 basketball trading cards.
    Joe gives him 18 more.
    How many basketball trading cards does
    Pedro have in all?

    Pedro has _____ basketball trading cards in all.

6.  Keisha has 15 stickers.
    She buys another 14 stickers.
    How many stickers does Keisha have in all?

    Keisha has _____ stickers in all.

**Solve.**

**Draw bar models to help you.**

**7.** Anna has 68 flowers.
She uses 56 flowers to make a garland.
How many flowers does Anna have now?

She has _____ flowers now.

**8.** There are 210 people in the theater.
Before the show begins, 162 more people
come into the theater.
How many people are in the theater now?

There are _____ people in the theater now.

# Lesson 3   Comparing Two Sets

**Solve.**
**Use the bar models to help you.**

1.  Eddie has 173 stamps.
    David has 68 more stamps than Eddie.
    How many stamps does David have?

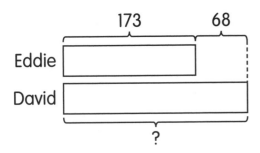

    David has _____ stamps.

2.  Susie has 235 red beads.
    She needs 47 fewer yellow beads than red beads
    to make a necklace.
    How many yellow beads does Susie need?

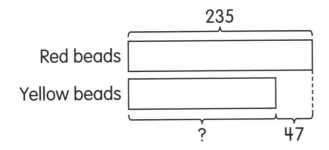

    Susie needs _____ yellow beads.

**Solve.**
**Draw bar models to help you.**

3. Daniel sells tickets to the fair to raise money.
   He sells 86 tickets on Monday.
   He sells 54 more tickets on Tuesday than on Monday.
   How many tickets does Daniel sell on Tuesday?

   Daniel sells _____ tickets on Tuesday.

4. Ali scores 345 points in a card game.
   Farid scores 89 points less than Ali.
   How many points does Farid score?

   Farid scores _____ points.

# Lesson 4   Real-World Problems: Two-Step Problems

**Solve.**
**Use the bar models to help you.**

1.    There are 36 sparrows and 18 crows on a tree.
     9 birds fly away.
     **a.**  How many birds were there at first?
     **b.**  How many birds are left?

**a.**

```
        36          18
     ┌────────────┬──────┐
     │            │      │
     └────────────┴──────┘
            ?
```

There were _____ birds at first.

**b.**

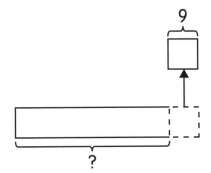

There are _____ birds left.

**Solve.**
**Use the bar models to help you.**

2.  Ivan spends $382 on food.
    He spends $235 more on clothes than he does on food.
    **a.** How much does Ivan spend on clothes?
    **b.** How much does Ivan spend in all?

    **a.**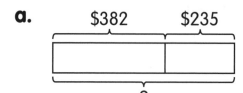

    Ivan spends $_____ on clothes.

    **b.**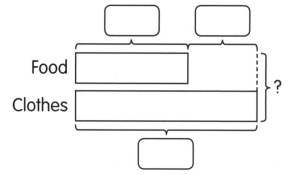

    Ivan spends $_____ in all.

# Solve.
## Draw bar models to help you.

3. Peter had 268 marbles.
   He put 128 red marbles in Box A.
   He put 76 blue marbles in Box B.
   Peter gave the remaining marbles to Jack.
   How many marbles did Peter give Jack?

First, find the total number of marbles in both the boxes.

Peter gave _____ marbles to Jack.

**Solve.**
**Draw bar models to help you.**

**4.**   Joel collects 286 stamps.
His brother James gives him 78 more stamps.
After that, Joel has 172 U.S. stamps.
The rest are stamps from Spain.
How many stamps from Spain does Joel have?

First, find out
how many stamps
Joel has in all.

Joel has _____ stamps from Spain.

 **Put on Your Thinking Cap!**

**Solve.**
**Draw bar models to help you.**

1. Ally has 5 crayons.
   Mike has 3 fewer crayons than Ally.
   Danny has 1 more crayon than Mike and Ally have in all.
   How many crayons do Danny, Ally, and Mike have in all?

They have _____ crayons in all.

**Solve.**

**2.** Sam has 21 students in his class.
7 of the students are boys.

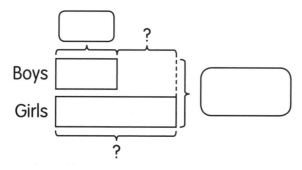

Read the sentences below.
Put a check (✓) in the box
next to the correct sentences.

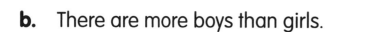

**a.** There are 7 more girls than boys.

**b.** There are more boys than girls.

**c.** There are 14 more girls than boys.

**d.** If 5 more boys join the class, there will be
2 more girls than boys in the class.

# CHAPTER 5 Multiplication and Division

## Lesson 1 How to Multiply

**Look at the pictures.**
**Fill in the blanks.**

**1.** A tricycle has 3 wheels.
How many wheels do 4 tricycles have?

4 threes = _____        $4 \times 3$ = _____

4 tricycles have _____ wheels.

**2.** There are 5 stars on each card.
How many stars are there on 10 cards?

10 fives = _____        $10 \times 5$ = _____

There are _____ stars on 10 cards.

**Count and add the number of balloons in each line.
Then multiply.**

**3.**

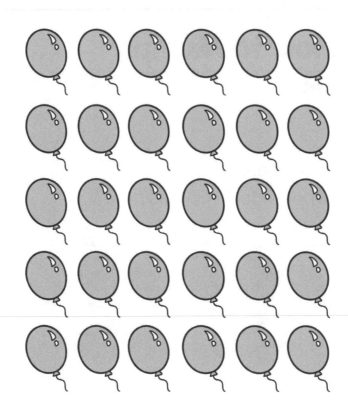

$6 + 6 + 6 + 6 + 6 =$ _____

_____ $\times\ 6 =$ _____

You can use repeated addition or multiplication to find the total number of things that are in equal groups.

**Look at the addition and multiplication sentences.**
**Fill in the blanks.**

4.      8 + 8 + 8 + 8 = 32
        4 × 8 = 32

Twyla has _____ groups of apples.

Each group has _____ apples.

There are _____ apples in all.

5.      7 + 7 + 7 = 21
        3 × 7 = 21

Louis has _____ groups of muffins.

Each group has _____ muffins.

There are _____ muffins in all.

**Write the multiplication sentences.**
**Fill in the blanks.**

**6.**   Vicky has 6 bracelets.
Each bracelet has 7 beads.

_____ × _____ = _____

There are _____ beads in all.

**7.**   Alex bought 4 bags of apples.
Each bag has 7 apples.

_____ × _____ = _____

There are _____ apples in all.

# Lesson 2   How to Divide

**Find the number of items in each group.**

1.    Divide 12 apples into 3 equal groups.

12 ÷ _____ = _____

There are _____ apples in each group.

2.    Divide 20 flowers into 5 equal groups.

20 ÷ _____ = _____

There are _____ flowers in each group.

## Find the number of groups.

**3.**    Divide 16 crackers into groups of 4.

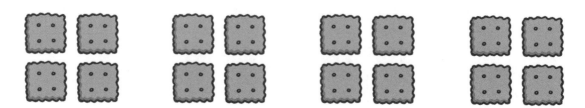

$16 \div$ _____ $=$ _____

There are _____ groups of 4 crackers.

**4.**    Divide 18 chicks into groups of 6.

$18 \div$ _____ $=$ _____

There are _____ groups of 6 chicks.

**Solve.**
**Use repeated subtraction to divide.**

**5.** Divide 15 balloons so there are 3 in each group.

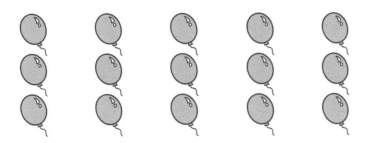

Subtract groups of 3 until there is nothing left.

15 – 3 – _____ – _____ – _____ – _____ = 0

15 ÷ 3 = _____

There are _____ groups.

**6.** Divide 21 worms so that each bird gets 7 worms.

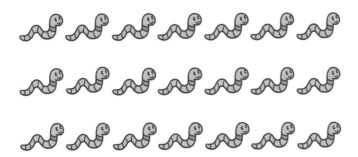

Subtract groups of 7 until there is nothing left.

21 – 7 – _____ – _____ = 0

21 ÷ 3 = _____

There are _____ groups of 7 worms.

Name: _____ Date: _____

## Solve.
## Use repeated subtraction to divide.

**7.** Divide 18 strawberries into groups of 9.

18 − _____ − _____ = 0

18 ÷ 9 = _____

There are _____ groups of 9 strawberries.

**8.** Divide 14 avocados into groups of 2.

14 − _____ − _____ − _____ − _____ −

_____ − _____ − _____ = 0

14 ÷ 2 = _____

There are _____ groups of 2 avocados.

# Lesson 3   Real-World Problems: Multiplication and Division

**Solve.**

1.  Felix has 3 fish bowls.
    Each bowl has 4 goldfish.
    How many goldfish does Felix have?

    _____ × _____ = _____

    Felix has _____ goldfish.

2.  I have 4 oranges.
    Each orange has 8 slices.
    How many slices do I have?

    _____ × _____ = _____

    I have _____ slices.

**Solve.**

3. There are 3 monkeys at the zoo.
   Sandra has 9 bananas to feed the monkeys.
   She gives each monkey an equal number of bananas.
   How many bananas does each monkey get?

_____ ÷ _____ = _____

Each monkey gets _____ bananas.

4. Nathan has 16 carrots.
   He gives 4 carrots to each of his pet rabbits.
   How many pet rabbits does he have?

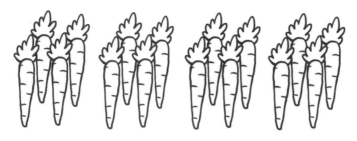

_____ ÷ _____ = _____

Nathan has _____ pet rabbits.

# Put on Your Thinking Cap!

1. Danny has 42 saplings.
He plants them equally in 8 rows.
How many saplings are left over?

_____ saplings are left over.

**2.** Fill in the blanks.

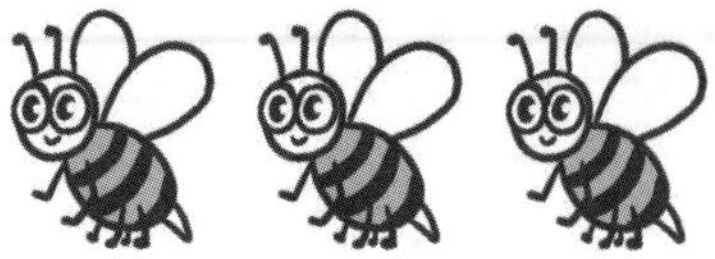

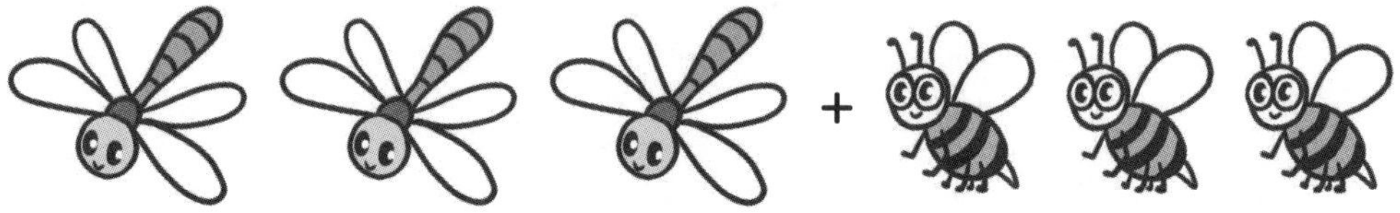

🐝🐝🐝 = 15

🪰🪰🪰 + 🐝🐝🐝 = 27

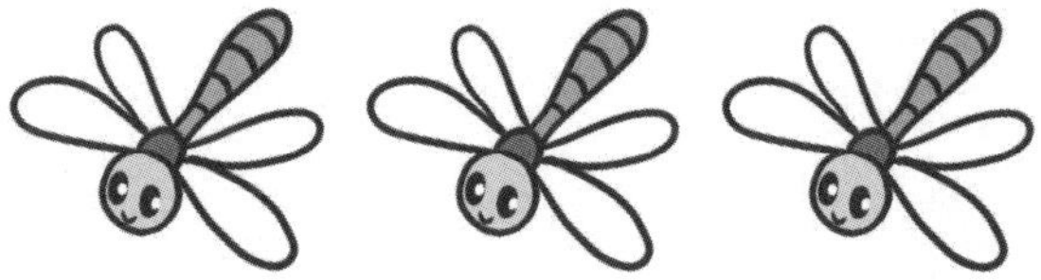

🪰🪰🪰 = _____

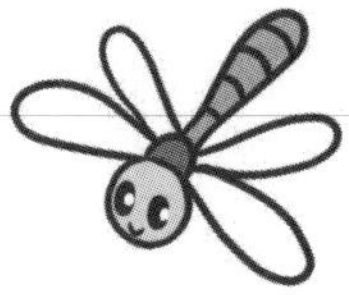

🪰 = _____

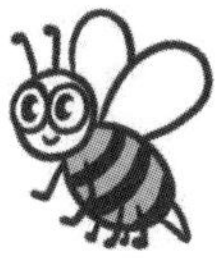

🐝 = _____

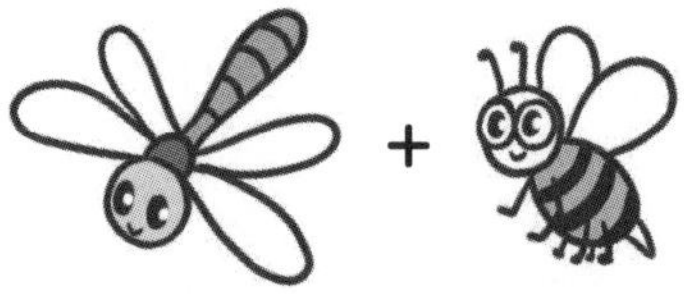

🪰 + 🐝 = _____

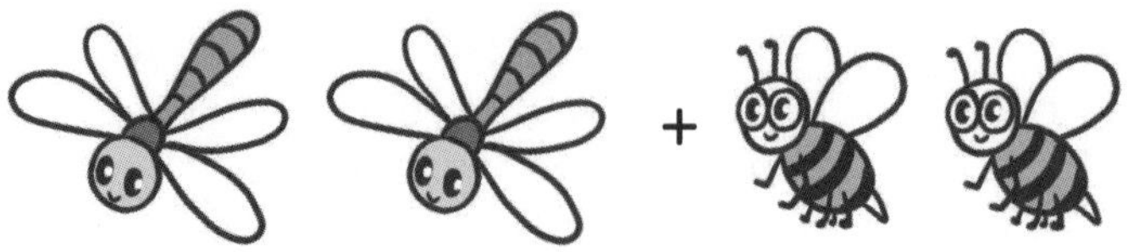

🪰🪰 + 🐝🐝 = _____

# CHAPTER 6 Multiplication Tables of 2, 5, and 10

## Lesson 1  Multiplying 2: Skip-Counting

**Count by 2s.**
**Then fill in the blanks.**

1. Each bicycle has 2 wheels.
   How many wheels do 8 bicycles have?

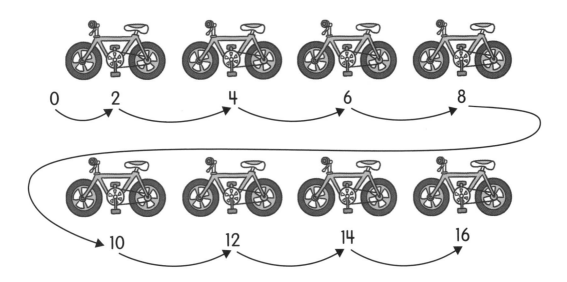

0 → 2 → 4 → 6 → 8 → 10 → 12 → 14 → 16

$8 \times 2 =$ _____

8 bicycles have _____ wheels.

**Count by 2s.**
**Color the fish that form a pattern.**
**Then fill in the blanks.**

**2.**

2, 4, _____, _____, _____, _____, _____

**Match.**

**3.**

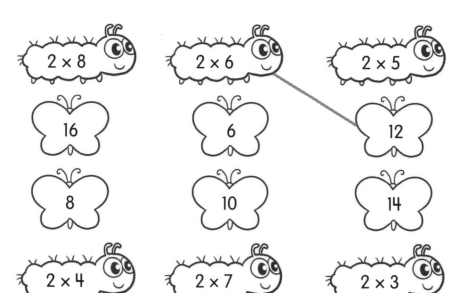

**Complete the table.**

**4.**

| Number of birds | 1 | 2 |   |   | 5 |   |   | 8 |   | 10 |
|---|---|---|---|---|---|---|---|---|---|---|
| Number of legs | 2 | 4 | 6 | 8 |   | 12 | 14 |   | 18 |   |

# Lesson 2   Multiplying 2: Using Dot Paper

**Use the dot paper to solve.**

1.  Mrs. Lee gives crackers to 8 children.
    Each child gets 2 crackers.
    How many crackers does Mrs. Lee
    give to the children in all?

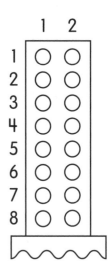

Mrs. Lee gives _____ crackers to the children in all.

2.  6 bicycles are in the shop.
    Each bicycle has 2 wheels.
    How many wheels are there in all?

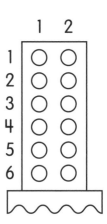

There are _____ wheels in all.

**Use the dot paper to fill in the blanks.**

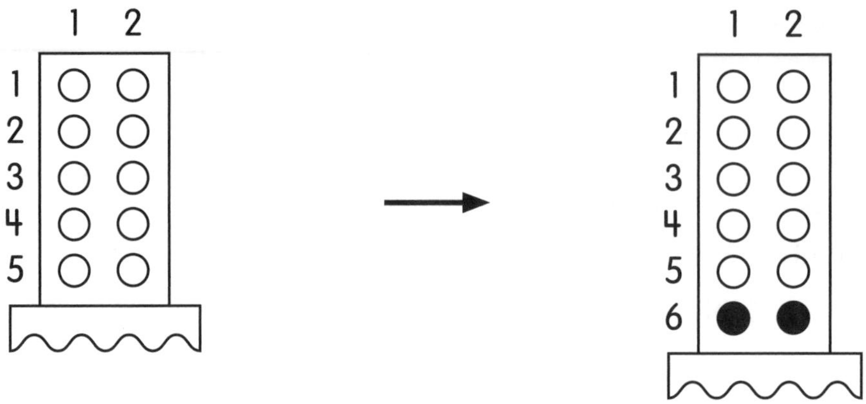

**3.**    $5 \times 2 =$ _____

**4.**    $6 \times 2 = 5 \times 2 +$ _____

**Use the dot paper to fill in the blanks.**

**5.**    $2 \times 2 = 1 \times 2 +$ _____ $\times 2$

   $= 2 +$ _____

   $=$ _____

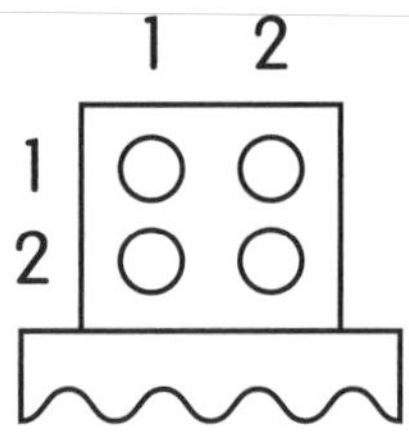

**6.**    $4 \times 2 = 1 \times 2 +$ _____ $\times 2$

   $= 2 +$ _____

   $=$ _____

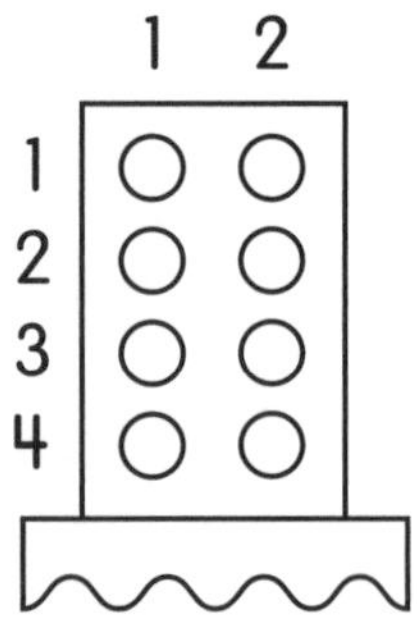

**Use the dot paper to fill in the blanks.**

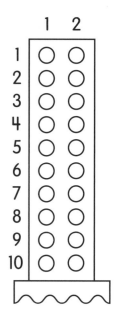

**7.**   5 × 2 is _____ more than 4 × 2.

**8.**   6 × 2 is _____ less than 9 × 2.

**9.**   9 × 2 is _____ more than 7 × 2.

**10.**   2 × 2 is _____ less than 8 × 2.

**Use the dot paper to find the missing numbers.**

**Example**

3 × 2 = _____6_____

2 × 3 = _____6_____

**11.**

5 × 2 = _____

2 × 5 = _____

**Use the dot paper to find the missing numbers.**

**12.**

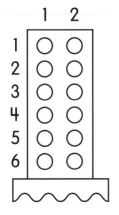

$6 \times 2 =$ _____

$2 \times 6 =$ _____

**13.**

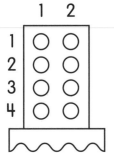

$4 \times 2 =$ _____

$2 \times 4 =$ _____

**14.**

$7 \times 2 =$ _____

$2 \times 7 =$ _____

# Lesson 3   Multiplying 5: Skip-Counting

**Count by 5s.**
**Then fill in the blanks.**

1.    5, _____, _____, _____, 25, _____

2.    25, _____, _____, 40, _____, _____

**Match.**

3.

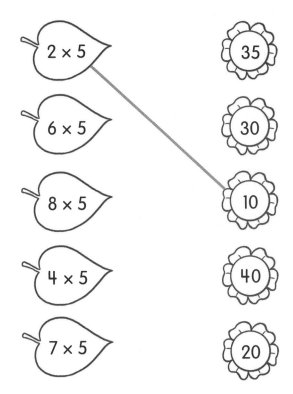

**Solve.**

4.  Mrs. Hill bakes 5 buns each day.
    How many buns does she bake in 6 days?

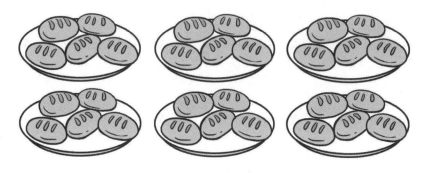

    6 × 5 = _____

    She bakes _____ buns in 6 days.

5.  Peter gives marbles to 7 friends.
    Each friend gets 5 marbles.
    How many marbles does Peter give his friends in all?

    _____ × _____ = _____

    Peter gives his friends _____ marbles in all.

# Lesson 4   Multiplying 5: Using Dot Paper

**Use the dot paper to solve.**

1.   There are 7 sheets of stickers.
     Each sheet has 5 stickers.
     How many stickers are there in all?

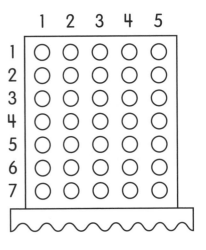

     There are _____ stickers in all.

2.   Sarah and her seven friends eat
     5 cherries each.
     How many cherries do they eat in all?

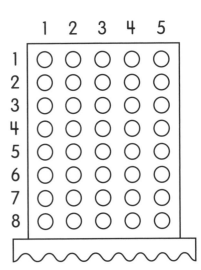

     They eat _____ cherries in all.

**Multiply.**
**Color the dots to help you.**

**3.**     3 × 5 = _____

**4.**     5 × 5 = _____

**Use the dot paper to fill in the blanks.**

**5.**     7 × 5 is _____ more than 6 × 5.

**6.**     10 × 5 is _____ more than 8 × 5.

**7.**     6 × 5 is _____ less than 8 × 5.

# Use the dot paper to fill in the blanks.

8.

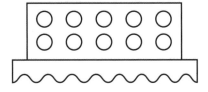

_____ × _____ = _____

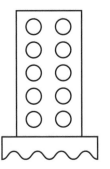

_____ × _____ = _____

9.

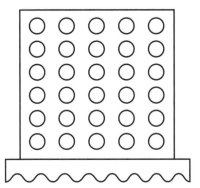

_____ × _____ = _____

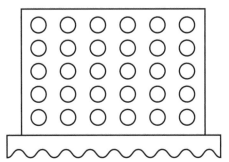

_____ × _____ = _____

**Use the dot paper to fill in the blanks.**

**10.**

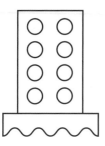

_____ × _____ = _____

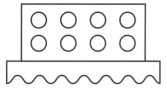

_____ × _____ = _____

**11.**

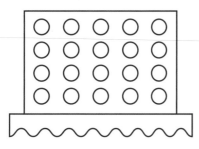

_____ × _____ = _____

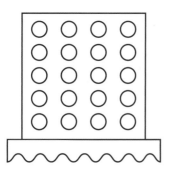

_____ × _____ = _____

# Lesson 5   Multiplying 10: Skip-Counting and Using Dot Paper

**Count by 10s.**
**Use some of the numbers to fill in the blanks.**

1.

10, 20, _____, 40, 50, _____, 70, 80, 90, _____

**Use patterns to fill in the blanks.**

2.   $8 \times 1 =$ _____

   $8 \times 10 =$ _____

3.   $9 \times 1 =$ _____

   $9 \times 10 =$ _____

4.   $10 \times 1 =$ _____

   $10 \times 10 =$ _____

**Solve.**

5. Eddie ties 4 bundles of balloons.
Each bundle has 10 balloons.
How many balloons are there in all?

There are _____ balloons in all.

6. Adena has 3 bracelets.
Each bracelet has 10 beads.
How many beads does Adena have in all?

Adena has _____ beads in all.

● **Solve.**

7. Kylie has 8 piles of books.
   Each pile has 10 books.
   How many books are there in all?

   There are _____ books in all.

8. Brooke buys 6 boxes of cards.
   Each box has 10 cards.
   How many cards does Brooke buy in all?

   Brooke buys _____ cards in all.

Name: _____ Date: _____

**Use the dot paper to multiply.**
**Complete the table.**

**9.**

|   | 1 | 2 | 3 | 4 | 5 | 6 | 7 | 8 | 9 | 10 |
|---|---|---|---|---|---|---|---|---|---|----|
| 1 | ○ | ○ | ○ | ○ | ○ | ○ | ○ | ○ | ○ | ○ |
| 2 | ○ | ○ | ○ | ○ | ○ | ○ | ○ | ○ | ○ | ○ |
| 3 | ○ | ○ | ○ | ○ | ○ | ○ | ○ | ○ | ○ | ○ |
| 4 | ○ | ○ | ○ | ○ | ○ | ○ | ○ | ○ | ○ | ○ |
| 5 | ○ | ○ | ○ | ○ | ○ | ○ | ○ | ○ | ○ | ○ |
| 6 | ○ | ○ | ○ | ○ | ○ | ○ | ○ | ○ | ○ | ○ |
| 7 | ○ | ○ | ○ | ○ | ○ | ○ | ○ | ○ | ○ | ○ |
| 8 | ○ | ○ | ○ | ○ | ○ | ○ | ○ | ○ | ○ | ○ |
| 9 | ○ | ○ | ○ | ○ | ○ | ○ | ○ | ○ | ○ | ○ |
| 10 | ○ | ○ | ○ | ○ | ○ | ○ | ○ | ○ | ○ | ○ |

There are 10 stamps in one box.

| Number of boxes | 3 | 6 | 7 | 8 | 10 |
|---|---|---|---|---|---|
| Number of stamps | 30 | | | | |

**10.**

|   | 1 | 2 | 3 | 4 | 5 | 6 | 7 | 8 | 9 | 10 |
|---|---|---|---|---|---|---|---|---|---|----|
| 1 | ○ | ○ | ○ | ○ | ○ | ○ | ○ | ○ | ○ | ○ |
| 2 | ○ | ○ | ○ | ○ | ○ | ○ | ○ | ○ | ○ | ○ |
| 3 | ○ | ○ | ○ | ○ | ○ | ○ | ○ | ○ | ○ | ○ |

|   | 1 | 2 | 3 |
|---|---|---|---|
| 1 | ○ | ○ | ○ |
| 2 | ○ | ○ | ○ |
| 3 | ○ | ○ | ○ |
| 4 | ○ | ○ | ○ |
| 5 | ○ | ○ | ○ |
| 6 | ○ | ○ | ○ |
| 7 | ○ | ○ | ○ |
| 8 | ○ | ○ | ○ |
| 9 | ○ | ○ | ○ |
| 10 | ○ | ○ | ○ |

$3 \times 10 =$ _____      $10 \times 3 =$ _____

# Lesson 6   Odd and Even Numbers

**Circle groups of 2.**
**Then fill in the blanks with *odd* or *even*.**

1.   There are 12 butterflies in a garden.

   12 is an _____ number.

2.   Louise has 15 dolls.

   15 is an _____ number.

3.   Leon bakes 21 muffins.

   21 is an _____ number.

4.   There are 30 fish in a pond.

   30 is an _____ number.

**Name:** _____ **Date:** _____

## Count by 2s.
## Then fill in the blanks with *odd* or *even*.

**5.**

9 is an _____ number.

**6.**

23 is an _____ number.

**7.**

34 is an _____ number.

**8.**

37 is an _____ number.

Name: _____   Date: _____

● **Fill in the blanks.**

**9.**  $14 =$ _____ $+$ _____

**10.**  $20 = 10 +$ _____

**11.**  _____ $= 14 + 14$

**12.**  $30 =$ _____ $+$ _____

**13.**  $36 =$ _____ $+$ _____

**14.**  $40 = 20 +$ _____

**15.**  _____ $= 24 + 24$

● **16.**  _____ $= 25 + 25$

**17.**  $62 =$ _____ $+$ _____

**18.**  $80 =$ _____ $+ 40$

**19.**  $86 =$ _____ $+$ _____

**20.**  $100 =$ _____ $+$ _____

Vicky has the digits 7, 5, 8, and 2.
Use the digits to help Vicky form the numbers below.
All the digits for each number must be different.

**21.**    the smallest 3-digit odd number _____

**22.**    the smallest 3-digit even number _____

**23.**    the greatest 3-digit odd number _____

**24.**    the greatest 3-digit even number _____

Megan has the digits 6, 0, 3, 1, and 9.
Use the digits to help Megan form the numbers below.
All the digits for each number must be different.

**25.**    the smallest 3-digit odd number _____

**26.**    the smallest 3-digit even number _____

**27.**    the greatest 3-digit odd number _____

**28.**    the greatest 3-digit even number _____

# Put on Your Thinking Cap!

1.  John thinks of two numbers.
    When he multiplies them, he gets 20.
    When he subtracts the smaller number from the
    bigger number, he gets 1.
    What are the two numbers?

Do you know what
my numbers are?

The two numbers are _____ and _____.

**2.** The shapes stand for different numbers.

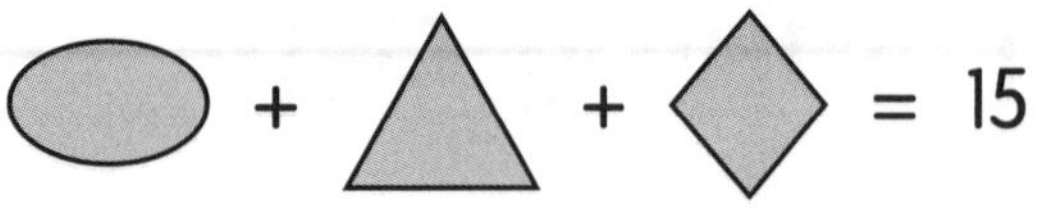

⬭ + △ + ◇ = 15

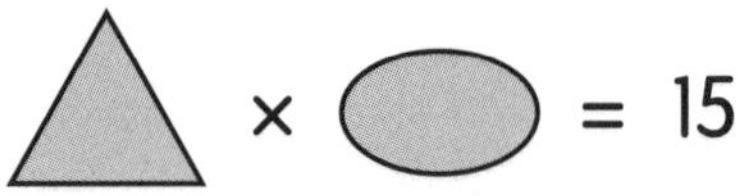

△ × ⬭ = 15

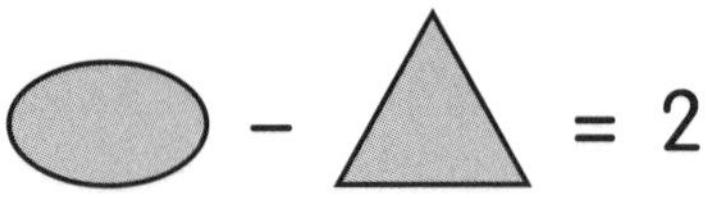

⬭ − △ = 2

**CLUES**

All the shapes stand for 1-digit odd numbers.
Odd numbers are numbers that are not found
in the multiplication table of 2.

Fill in the boxes with the correct answers.

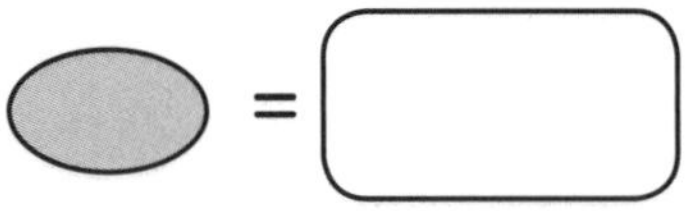

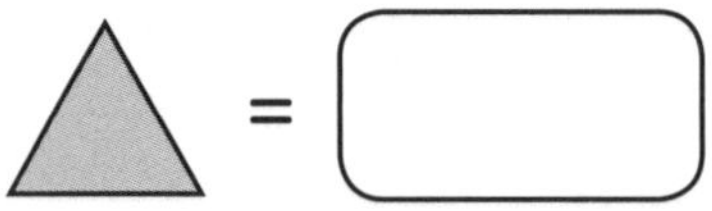

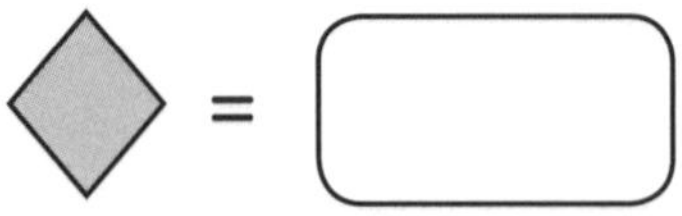

⬭ = ☐          △ = ☐

◇ = ☐

## Test Prep

$\boxed{\diagup\ 80}$

**for Chapters 1 to 6**

# Multiple Choice (10 × 2 points = 20 points)

**Fill in the circle next to the correct answer.**

1. Seven hundred fifty-two is written as _____.

   (A) 752      (B) 705      (C) 572      (D) 527

2. 4 tens and 9 tens make _____.

   (A) 1 hundred and 3 tens

   (B) 13 hundreds

   (C) 1 hundred and 2 tens

   (D) 14 hundreds

3. 324 is 10 less than _____.

   (A) 304      (B) 314      (C) 334      (D) 343

4. Which is the greatest number?

   ## 345 626 809 799

   (A) 809      (B) 345      (C) 799      (D) 626

5. 856 + 114 = _____

   (A) 980      (B) 970      (C) 962      (D) 907

**6.** 700 − 419 = _____

(A) 271          (B) 281          (C) 290          (D) 319

**7.** There are 3 plates of apples on the table.
Each plate contains 5 apples.
How many apples are there in all?

(A) 3 + 5 = 8

(B) 3 × 5 = 15

(C) 3 × 3 = 9

(D) 15 ÷ 3 = 5

## Use the bar model to answer Exercises 8 and 9.

Chickens | 35
Rabbits | 15
} ?

**8.** There are _____ more chickens than rabbits.

(A) 50          (B) 35          (C) 20          (D) 15

**9.** There are _____ animals on the farm in all.

(A) 80          (B) 70          (C) 55          (D) 50

**10.** Divide 18 oranges into 3 equal groups.

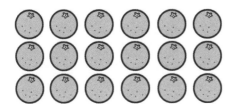

There are _____ oranges in each group.

Ⓐ  5            Ⓑ  6            Ⓒ  7            Ⓓ  18

# Short Answer (10 × 2 points = 20 points)

**Follow the directions.**

**11.**  **a.**  Write the value of 8 hundreds and 3 ones. _____

**b.**  Add and subtract mentally.

$8 + 6 =$ _____

$13 + 7 =$ _____

**12.**  Fill in the blanks.

**a.**  236 = 2 hundreds 3 tens and _____ ones

= 2 hundreds 2 tens and _____ ones

**b.**  516 = _____ hundreds 1 ten and 6 ones

= 4 hundreds _____ tens and 6 ones

**13.**   Use each digit once to form the greatest 3-digit number.

# 8  3  9

_____

## Complete the patterns.
## Fill in the missing numbers.

**14.**   **a.**

264 | 364 | 464 | | |

**b.**

685 | 584 | 483 | | |

**15.**   Order the numbers from least to greatest.

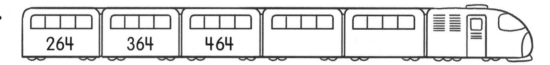

_____, _____, _____, _____, _____
   least

**16.**   Add 324 to 82.

_____

**17.**   Subtract 74 from 107.

_____

**18.** Use the numbers to form number sentences.

**a.** 305, 420, 115

**b.** 152, 227, 75

**19.** Divide 21 fish into 3 equal groups.
Then fill in the missing numbers.

$21 \div 3 =$ _____

Each group will have _____ fish.

**20.** Justin has 25 marbles.
He divides the marbles equally into 5 bags.
How many marbles are in each bag?

_____ marbles are in each bag.

# Extended Response (8 × 5 points = 40 points)

## Solve.
## Use the bar models to help you.

21.  There are 228 boys and 196 girls in a school.
     How many students are there in all?

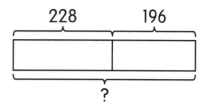

     There are _____ students in all.

22.  Jose and Lin have 237 marbles in all.
     Lin has 82 marbles.
     How many marbles does Jose have?

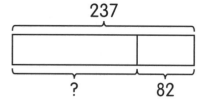

     Jose has _____ marbles.

**23.** June has 134 toy animals.
Her brother buys her 27 more toy animals.
How many toy animals does June have in all?

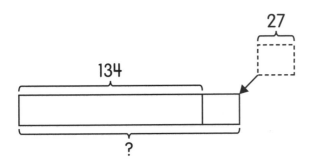

June has _____ toy animals in all.

**24.** Fabriz has 367 green beads for a craft project.
He needs 103 more green beads.
How many green beads does Fabriz need for this project?

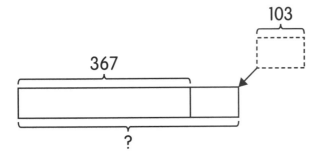

Fabriz needs _____ green beads for his project.

**Solve.**

**Use the bar models to help you.**

25.   A tree farm has 140 pine trees.
      The farm sells some of them and has 61 trees left.
      How many trees did the farm sell?

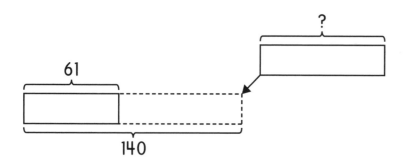

The farm sold _____ trees.

26.   245 people attend the opera on Saturday.
      During the break, 37 people left.
      How many people were left at the opera?

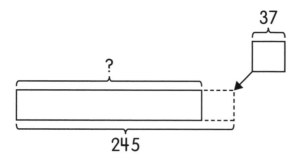

_____ people were still at the opera.

**27.** There are 64 cows and 26 sheep at Dairy Farm A.
There are 37 fewer animals at Dairy Farm B.
   **a.** How many animals are there at Dairy Farm A?
   **b.** How many animals are there at Dairy Farm B?

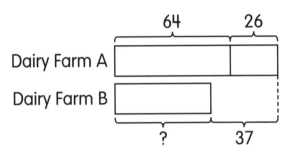

**a.**




There are _____ animals at Dairy Farm A.

**b.**




There are _____ animals at Dairy Farm B.

**Solve.**

**Use the bar models to help you.**

**28.**   Lily sells 358 tickets in the morning.
         She sells 185 tickets in the afternoon.
         She has 131 tickets left.
         **a.**   How many tickets did Lily sell?
         **b.**   How many tickets did Lily have in all?

**a.**

| 358 | 185 |
|-----|-----|
|     |     |

?

Lily sold _____ tickets.

**b.**

| ? | 131 |
|---|-----|

?

Lily had _____ tickets in all.

# CHAPTER 7 Metric Measurement of Length

## Lesson 1   Measuring in Meters

**Look at the pictures.**
**Fill in the blanks with *more* or *less*.**

**1.**

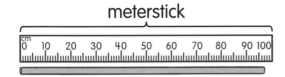

meterstick

The length of the rod is _____ than 1 meter.

**2.**

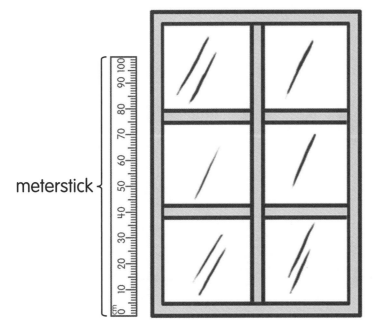

meterstick

The height of the window is _____ than 1 meter.

**3.**

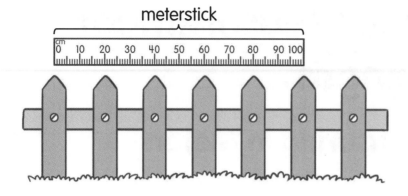

The length of the fence is _____ than 1 meter.

**4.**

The height of the lamp is _____ than 1 meter.

Name: _____ Date: _____

● Look at the list below.
Check (✔) the columns that are true.
You will need a meterstick or a 1-meter string to measure some objects.

5.

| Object | Less than 1 meter | More than 1 meter | More than 1 meter but less than 2 meters | More than 2 meters |
|---|---|---|---|---|
| **a.** a bus | | | | |
| **b.** a fan | | | | |
| **c.** a keyboard | | | | |
| **d.** a sofa | | | | |

**Circle the objects that are about 1 meter long.**

**6.**

a see-saw

a television set

**7.**

a bed

a monitor

# Lesson 2   Comparing Lengths in Meters

**Fill in the blanks.**

1.   Look at the two strings of beads.

   **3 m**            **2 m**
   **String A**       **String B**

   a.   Which string of beads is longer? String _____

   b.   How much longer is it? _____ m

2.   Look at the two penguins.

   **4 m**            **2 m**
   **Penguin A**      **Penguin B**

   a.   Which penguin is taller? Penguin _____

   b.   How much taller is it? _____ m

**Fill in the blanks.**

**3.**   Look at the sides of the door.

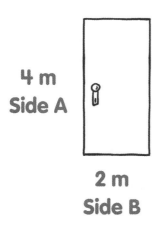

4 m
Side A

2 m
Side B

**a.**   Which is shorter, Side A or Side B? Side _____

**b.**   How much shorter is it? _____ m

**4.**   Look at the trees.

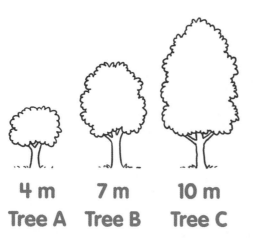

4 m       7 m       10 m
Tree A   Tree B   Tree C

**a.**   Which tree is the tallest? Tree _____

**b.**   Which tree is the shortest? Tree _____

**c.**   Tree A is _____ meters shorter than Tree B.

**d.**   Tree C is _____ meters taller than Tree A.

# Lesson 3   Measuring in Centimeters

**Use your centimeter ruler to draw.**

**1.**   a line that is 4 centimeters long

**2.**   a line that is 2 centimeters longer than the line in Exercise 1

## Use a centimeter ruler to find the length of the drawings.

**3.**   _____
        Drawing A

**4.**   _____
        Drawing B

**5.**   _____
        Drawing C

## Fill in the missing numbers.

**6.**

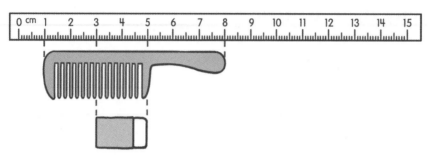

The eraser is about _____ centimeters long.

The toy comb is about _____ centimeters long.

**7.**

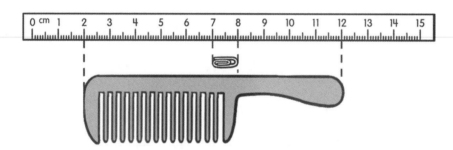

The paperclip is about _____ centimeter long.

The comb is about _____ centimeters long.

These rulers are smaller than in real life.

© Marshall Cavendish International (Singapore) Private Limited.

# Lesson 4   Comparing Lengths in Centimeters

**Fill in the blanks.**

1.   Line A

Line B

Line C

Line _____ is the longest.

Line _____ is the shortest.

Line _____ is longer than Line _____,

but shorter than Line _____.

**Measure the lengths of the pencils.**
**Use a centimeter ruler.**
**Then fill in the blanks.**

2.   Pencil A                                   _____ cm

Pencil B                                _____ cm

Pencil C                                _____ cm

Pencil D                                   _____ cm

3.   Pencil D is _____ centimeters longer than Pencil A.

4.   Pencil B is _____ centimeters shorter than Pencil C.

**Fill in the missing numbers.**

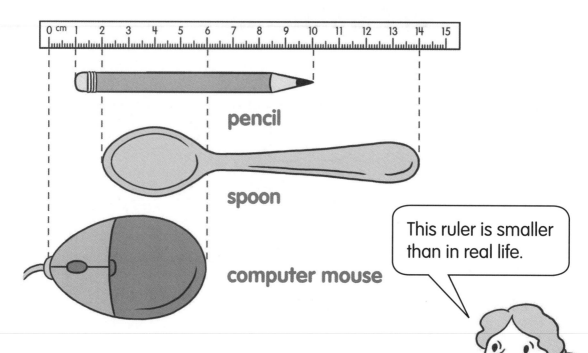

5.  The pencil is about _____ centimeters long.

6.  The computer mouse is about _____ centimeters long.

7.  The spoon is about _____ centimeters long.

**Use your answers in Exercises 5 to 7.**
**Fill in the blanks with *longer* or *shorter*.**

8.  The pencil is _____ than the computer mouse.

9.  The spoon is _____ than the pencil.

10. The computer mouse is _____ than the spoon.

# Lesson 5  Real-World Problems: Metric Length

**Solve.**

1.  Timothy has 24 meters of ribbon.
    He cuts it into 2 pieces.
    The shorter piece is 6 meters long.
    What is the length of the longer piece?

    The length of the longer piece is _____ meters.

2.  Mrs. Hall has two closets.
    One of them is 90 centimeters wide.
    The other closet is 121 centimeters wide.
    They are placed side by side.
    What is the total width of the two closets?

    The total width of the two closets is _____ centimeters.

**3.** Mrs. Feliciano has 10 meters of cloth.
She uses 3 meters of cloth to sew a tablecloth.
She uses the rest of the cloth to sew some curtains.
What is the length of cloth Mrs. Feliciano uses
to sew curtains?

Mrs. Feliciano uses _____ meters of cloth to sew curtains.

**4.** Keenan has 30 centimeters of lace.
He cuts it into two pieces.
The length of the first piece is 12 centimeters.
How much shorter is the first piece than the second piece?

The first piece is _____ centimeters shorter than the
second piece.

**5.** Minnie is 139 centimeters tall.
Stuart is 15 centimeters taller than Minnie.
How tall is Stuart?

Stuart is _____ centimeters tall.

**6.** The model railway track from Town A to Town B is
400 meters long.
The model railway track from Town B to Town C is
129 meters long.
What is the length of the model railway track from Town A
to Town C?

The length of the model railway track from Town A to Town C

is _____ meters.

**7.** Julius has a string of lights that is 500 centimeters long.
He uses 45 centimeters to decorate the front door.
His sister uses 125 centimeters to decorate her room.
How long is the string of lights that Julius has left?

The length of the string of lights that Julius has left is

_____ centimeters.

**8.**    Sarah is 119 centimeters tall.
Bernice is 21 centimeters taller than Sarah.
Fiona is 11 centimeters shorter than Bernice.
How tall is Fiona?

Fiona is _____ centimeters tall.

**9.**  Zachary has a toy train that is 60 centimeters long.
His aunt buys him a new toy train that is 85 centimeters longer.

    **a.**  What is the length of the new toy train?

        The length of the new toy train is _____ centimeters.

    **b.**  What is the length of both the toy trains in all?

        The length of both the toy trains is _____ centimeters in all.

 Put on Your Thinking Cap!

1.      John has 4 sticks.
        He orders them from longest to shortest.
        Stick C is between Stick A and Stick D.
        Stick C is longer than Stick A.
        Stick A is longer than Stick B.

        **a.**  Which stick is the shortest?

                Stick _____ is the shortest.

        **b.**  Which stick is the longest?

                Stick _____ is the longest.

2.      Aiesha uses building blocks to make a train.
        She has 10-centimeter and 20-centimeter building blocks.
        The total length of the train is 50-centimeters.
        How many 10-centimeter and 20-centimeter building blocks
        did Aiesha use?
        Show all possible answers.

**Name:** _____ **Date:** _____

## Use the clues and pictures to help you complete the table.

3. Azura strings beads together to form bracelets.
   Each bracelet is a different color.
   What is the color of each bracelet?
   How many beads are used to string each bracelet?

> **CLUES**
> Azura uses 32 red beads.
> She uses 9 fewer yellow beads than red beads.
> She uses 2 more green beads than yellow beads.
> She uses 3 more blue beads than red beads.

Bracelet A  —〜〜〜〜〜〜〜〜〜〜〜〜〜〜〜—

Bracelet B  —〜〜〜〜〜〜〜〜〜〜〜〜〜〜〜〜—

Bracelet C  —〜〜〜〜〜〜〜〜〜〜〜—

Bracelet D  —〜〜〜〜〜〜〜〜〜〜—

| Bracelet | Color | Number of beads used |
|----------|-------|---------------------|
| Bracelet A | | |
| Bracelet B | | |
| Bracelet C | | |
| Bracelet D | | |

CHAPTER

# 8  Mass

## Lesson 1   Measuring in Kilograms

**Fill in the blanks.**

**1.**

| more than |
| less than |
| as heavy as |

The mass of the bag of sugar is _____ 1 kilogram.

**2.**

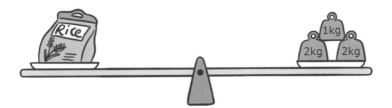

The mass of the bag of rice is _____ 1 kilogram.

**3.**

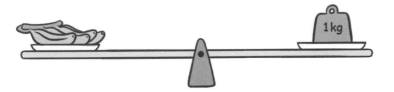

The mass of the bananas is _____ 1 kilogram.

**Read the scales.**
**Then fill in the blanks.**

**4.**

tomatoes

The mass of the tomatoes is _____ kilograms.

**5.**

fruit juice

The mass of the fruit juice is _____ kilogram.

**6.**

celery

The mass of the celery is _____ kilograms.

# Lesson 2   Comparing Masses in Kilograms

**Look at the pictures.**
**Then answer the questions.**

8 kg

suitcase

4 kg

chair

6 kg

bicycle

1 kg

lamp

1.   The _____ is the heaviest.

2.   The _____ is the lightest.

3.   The _____ is lighter than the chair.

4.   The _____ is heavier than the bicycle.

## Write the mass.

**5.** 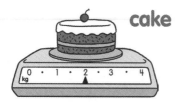 cake

_____ kg

**6.**  tomatoes

_____ kg

**7.**  Mr. Clark

_____ kg

**8.**  Emily

_____ kg

## Fill in the blanks.
## Use your answers in Exercises 5 to 8 to help you.

**9.** Which is the lightest? _____

**10.** Which is the heaviest? _____

**11.** The cake is _____ kilograms lighter than the tomatoes.

**12.** Order the objects from heaviest to lightest.

_____, _____, _____, _____
heaviest

# Lesson 3   Measuring in Grams

**Read the scales.**
**Then write the mass.**

1.

grapes

☐ g

2.

orange

☐ g

3.

apples

☐ g

4.

pineapple

☐ g

**Fill in the blanks.**

**5.**

 cucumber

 broccoli

The cucumber has a mass of _____ grams.

The broccoli has a mass of _____ grams.

**6.**

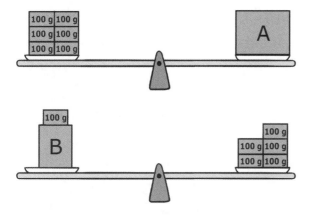

The mass of Box A is _____ grams.

The mass of Box B is _____ grams.

Box _____ is lighter than Box _____.

# Lesson 4   Comparing Masses in Grams

**Look at the pictures.**
**Then fill in the blanks.**

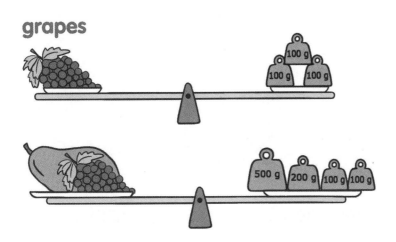

grapes

1.   The mass of the grapes is _____ grams.

2.   The mass of the papaya is _____ grams.

3.   The _____ is heavier than the _____.

**Fill in the blank with *heavier* or *lighter*.**

4.

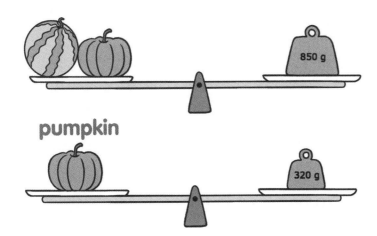

pumpkin

The watermelon is _____ than the pumpkin.

**Fill in the blanks.**

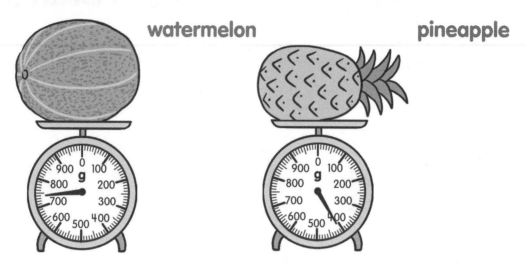

watermelon                    pineapple

5.    The mass of the watermelon is _____ grams.

6.    The mass of the pineapple is _____ grams.

7.    The _____ is lighter than the _____.

**Compare the masses of the four packages.**

8.

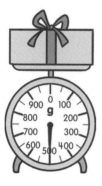   

Package A        Package B        Package C        Package D

Order the packages from heaviest to lightest.

_____, _____, _____, _____
    heaviest

# Lesson 5   Real-World Problems: Mass

**Solve.**
**Use bar models to help you.**

1.      Mrs. Herrera has two cats.
        The masses of the two cats are 4 kilograms and 5 kilograms.
        What is the total mass of the two cats?

        The total mass of the two cats is _____ kilograms.

2.      Sally bakes 500 grams of bread.
        She gives 127 grams of bread to her neighbor.
        What is the mass of the bread that is left?

        The mass of the bread that is left is _____ grams.

**3.**      Leanne has a mass of 25 kilograms.
         She is 8 kilograms heavier than Stella.
         What is Stella's mass?

         Stella's mass is _____ kilograms.

**4.**      Mr. Vasquez buys 900 grams of flour.
         He uses 225 grams of flour to make pumpkin bread.
         He uses 150 grams of flour to make carrot muffins.
         What is the mass of flour Mr. Vasquez has left?

         The mass of flour Mr. Vasquez has left is _____ grams.

**5.** A grocer sells 35 kilograms of potatoes on Tuesday.
He sells 23 kilograms more potatoes on Wednesday
than on Tuesday.
How many kilograms of potatoes does he sell in all?

He sells _____ kilograms of potatoes in all.

**6.** Mr. Dane has a mass of 87 kilograms.
Bobby's mass is 48 kilograms less than Mr. Dane's mass.
What is the total mass of Bobby and Mr. Dane?

The total mass of Bobby and Mr. Dane is _____ kilograms.

## Put on Your Thinking Cap!

1.   The mass of 2 [            ] is the same as the mass of 3 [       ].

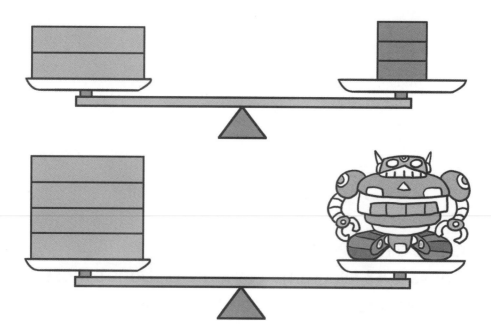

The mass of the robot is equal to 4 [              ].

The mass of the robot also equals _____ [      ].

# CHAPTER  9 Volume

## Lesson 1   Getting to Know Volume

**Circle the correct answer.**

1.    Which container holds more water?

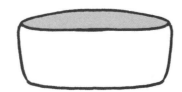

2.    Which container holds less water?

3.    Which container holds the least amount of water?

**4.**   Which container holds the greatest amount of water?

**Look at the pictures.**
**Then fill in the blanks.**

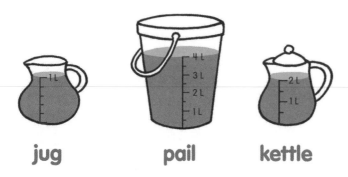

jug        pail        kettle

**5.**   The _____ has the least amount of water.

**6.**   The _____ has the greatest amount of water.

Name: _____ Date: _____

## Fill in the blanks.

Susan fills glasses of the same size with all the water
from Containers A, B, and C.

**Container A**

**Container B**

**Container C**

**7.** Container _____ had more water than Container C.

**8.** Container _____ had the greatest amount of water.

**9.** Container _____ had the least amount of water.

**10.** Order Containers A, B, and C.
Begin with the container that had the greatest amount of water.

_____, _____, _____
        most

**Fill in the blanks.**

Calvin fills glasses of the same size with all the water
from the containers.

pot

watering can

jug

kettle

11.    The _____ had the greatest amount of water.

12.    The _____ had the least amount of water.

13.    The jug had _____ fewer glasses of water than the
       watering can.

14.    The pot had _____ more glasses of water than the kettle.

# Lesson 2  Measuring in Liters

**Find the volume of water in each container.**

**Example**

Volume of water = __4 liters__ or __4 L__

**1.**

Volume of water = _____ or _____

**2.**

Volume of water = _____ or _____

**3.**

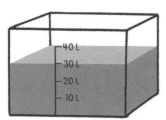

Volume of water = _____ or _____

## Check (✔) the box if the sentence is true.

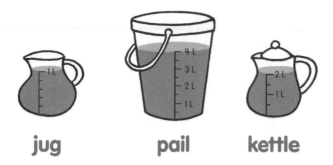

jug        pail        kettle

**4.** The jug has more than 2 liters of water.    ☐

     The pail has more water than the kettle.    ☐

     The kettle has more than 2 liters of water.    ☐

     The pail has the greatest amount of water.    ☐

## Fill in the blanks.

**5.** All the water in the jug is poured into the bottles.

 ➡

The volume of water in the jug was _____ liters.

**6.** All the water in the pail is poured into the jugs.

 ➡

The volume of water in the pail was _____ liters.

## Fill in the blanks.

**7.** All the water in the bottle is poured into the beakers.

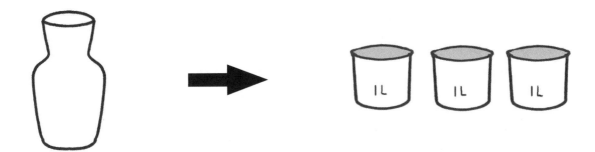

The bottle had _____ liters of water at first.

**8.** All the orange juice in the jug is poured into the glasses.

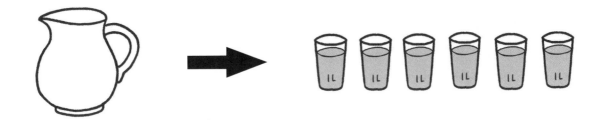

The jug had _____ liters of orange juice at first.

**9.** All the water in the pan is poured into the bottles.

The pan had _____ liters of water at first.

**Fill in the blanks.**

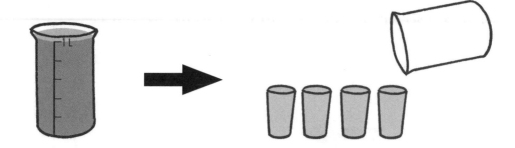

10. The volume of water in the beaker is the same as the

    volume of water in _____ glasses.

11. Four glasses have _____ liter of water in all.

**Fill in the blanks.**

| bottles | pot | mugs |
|---------|-----|------|
| 1 liter of water | 1 liter of water | 1 liter of water |

12. Order a bottle, a pot, and a mug.
    Begin with the container that has the most amount of water.

    _____, _____, _____
    most

# Lesson 3  Real-World Problems: Volume

**Solve.**
**Draw bar models to help you.**

1.  A tank contains 26 liters of water.
    Peter pours another 18 liters of water into the tank.
    How much water does the tank contain now?

    The tank contains _____ liters of water now.

2.  Mrs. Lee makes some fruit punch for a party.
    After serving 19 liters of fruit punch, she has
    28 liters of fruit punch left.
    How many liters of fruit punch did Mrs. Lee make at first?

    Mrs. Lee made _____ liters of fruit punch at first.

3.    A dairy farm sells 76 liters of milk on Monday.
      It sells 94 liters of milk on Tuesday.
      How much more milk was sold on Tuesday than on Monday?

            _____ liters more milk were sold on Tuesday than
      on Monday.

4.    There are 42 liters of water in a tank.
      Michael waters the garden with some water from the tank.
      27 liters of water are left in the tank.
      How much water did Michael use?

            Michael used _____ liters of water.

 Put on Your Thinking Cap!

**1.** How many bottles of water are needed to fill the beaker?

**beaker**                           **bottle**

_____ bottles of water are needed to fill the beaker.

**2.** Sue fills a pail completely with 4 liters of water.
Each time she pours the pail of water into a tank,
she spills 1 liter of water.
Sue pours 15 liters of water into the tank.
How many pails of water does Sue use?

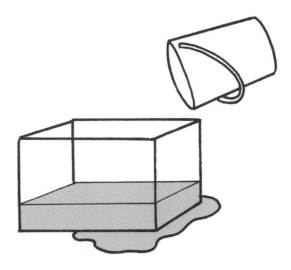

She uses _____ pails of water.

**3.** Amy has a pail that can hold 5 liters, one that holds 3 liters, and one that holds 1 liter of water.

She uses these three pails to fill up Container A, Container B, and Container C.

What is the least number of pails of water that she will need?

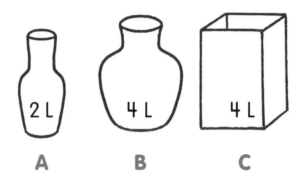

A          B          C

The least number of pails of water that she needs is _____.

# Mid-Year Test Prep

## Multiple Choice (20 × 2 points = 40 points)

**Fill in the circle next to the correct answer.**

1. 700 + _____ + 2 = 792

   (A) 2  (B) 9  (C) 70  (D) 90

2. 10 less than 268 is _____.

   (A) 168  (B) 258  (C) 278  (D) 368

3. 625 + 285 = _____

   (A) 910  (B) 905  (C) 900  (D) 340

4. Jim has 67 stamps.
   Peter has 19 stamps.
   How many stamps do they have in all?

   (A) 96  (B) 89  (C) 86  (D) 48

5. 325 − 64 = _____

   (A) 126  (B) 216  (C) 261  (D) 389

6. 48 + 76 = _____

   (A) 115  (B) 124  (C) 126  (D) 148

**7.** The table shows the number of apples on each tree.

| Tree | A | B | C | D |
|---|---|---|---|---|
| Number of apples | 122 | 106 | 78 | 100 |

Which two trees have 200 apples in all?

(A) A and B          (B) A and C

(C) A and D          (D) B and C

**8.** Arrange 18 party hats in groups of 2.
How many groups of party hats are there?

(A) 10          (B) 9          (C) 8          (D) 7

**9.** If ☆ + ☆ + ☆ + ☆ + ☆ = 45,

☆ stands for _____.

(A) 9          (B) 6          (C) 3          (D) 4

**10.**

3 sixes = _____ or 3 × 6 = _____

(A) 5        (B) 6        (C) 3        (D) 18

**11.** Roy gave 15 stickers to Joel.
He gave two times as many stickers to Tracey.
How many stickers did Roy give to Tracey?

(A) 30        (B) 40        (C) 50        (D) 60

**12.** Which crayon has the shortest length?

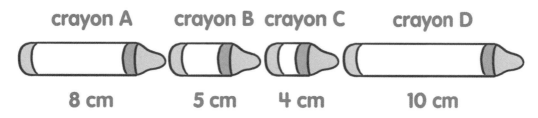

crayon A    crayon B   crayon C     crayon D

8 cm     5 cm    4 cm     10 cm

(A) crayon A

(B) crayon B

(C) crayon C

(D) crayon D

**13.** Rachel is 152 centimeters tall.
Her brother is 48 centimeters shorter than she is.
How tall is Rachel's brother?

Ⓐ 104 cm

Ⓑ 114 cm

Ⓒ 140 cm

Ⓓ 200 cm

**14.** The papaya has a mass of about _____ grams.

Ⓐ 100      Ⓑ 104      Ⓒ 140      Ⓓ 150

**15.** Mrs. Diaz needs 250 grams of sugar to make bran muffins.
She has only 185 grams of sugar.
How much more sugar does Mrs. Diaz need?

Ⓐ 60 grams

Ⓑ 65 grams

Ⓒ 425 grams

Ⓓ 435 grams

Use the pictures to answer Exercises 16 to 18.
The mass of each ▭ is 100 grams.

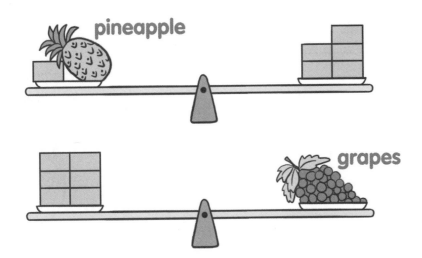
pineapple

grapes

16. The mass of the grapes is _____ grams.

    Ⓐ 600      Ⓑ 500      Ⓒ 350      Ⓓ 300

17. The mass of the pineapple is _____ grams.

    Ⓐ 200      Ⓑ 250      Ⓒ 300      Ⓓ 400

18. The grapes are _____ than the pineapple

    by _____ grams.

    Ⓐ heavier, 200      Ⓑ lighter, 200

    Ⓒ heavier, 300      Ⓓ lighter, 400

**Name:** _____   **Date:** _____

19.

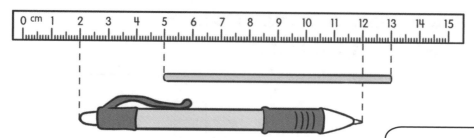

This ruler is smaller than in real life.

The pen is _____ centimeters long.

(A)  12

(B)  11

(C)  10

(D)  8

20.

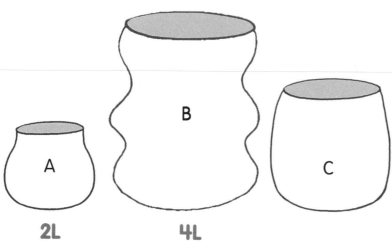

2L       4L

Sue has three containers.
Container A can hold 2 liters of water.
Container B can hold 4 liters of water.
Container C can hold less water than Container B,
but more water than Container A.
How much water can Container C hold?

(A)  1 liter

(B)  2 liters

(C)  3 liters

(D)  4 liters

# Short Answer (20 x 2 points = 40 points)

**Follow the directions.**

**21.** Order the numbers from greatest to least.

_____, _____, _____, _____
greatest

**22.** Fill in the blanks with *greater* or *less*.

**a.** 255 is _____ than 325.

**b.** 720 is _____ than 702.

**23.** Write the numbers in word form.

**a.** 648 _____

**b.** 302 _____

**24.** Add and subtract mentally.

**a.** 9 + 8 = _____

**b.** 16 − 9 = _____

**25.** **a.** Add 248 and 356. _____

**b.** Subtract 250 from 501. _____

**26.** How many cars are there in all?

_____ × _____ = _____

There are _____ cars in all.

**27.** Katia has a handkerchief and a face towel.
She puts them next to each other.
What is the length of the face towel?

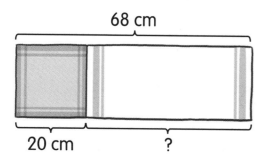

The length of the face towel is _____ centimeters.

**28.**

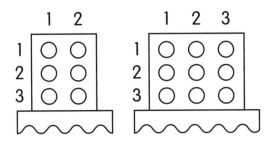

$3 \times 2$ is _____ less than $3 \times 3$.

**29.** Each toy bicycle has 2 wheels.
How many wheels do 4 toy bicycles have?

4 toy bicycles have _____ wheels.

**30.** 2 boys share 16 pencils equally.

$16 \div 2 =$ _____

Each boy gets _____ pencils.

**31.**  What is the mass of the apple?

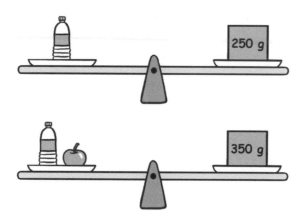

The mass of the apple is _____ grams.

**32.**  Complete the number patterns.

**a.**  12, 14, _____, 18, _____, 22

**b.**  10, 15, _____, _____, 30, 35

**33.**  Measure the straws shown below.
Use a centimeter ruler.
Then fill in the blanks.

Straw A

Straw B

Straw C

Straw A is _____ centimeters long.

Straw B is _____ centimeters long.

Straw C is _____ centimeters long.

**34.**

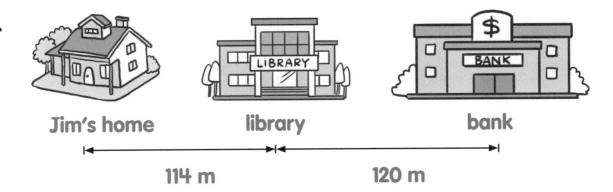

| Jim's home | library | bank |
|---|---|---|

114 m     120 m

Jim's home is 114 meters from the library.
The library is 120 meters from the bank.
How far is the bank from Jim's home?

The bank is _____ meters from Jim's home.

**Use the pictures to answer Exercises 35 to 37.**

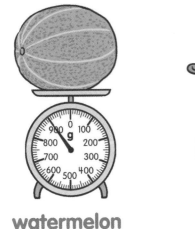   

**watermelon**      **bananas**      **chicken**      **fish**

**35.** The mass of the watermelon is _____ grams.

**36.** The mass of the bananas is _____ grams.

**37.** The chicken is _____ grams heavier than the fish.

**38.**     368 = 3 hundreds _____ tens 8 ones

= 2 hundreds _____ tens 8 ones

**39.**

1 bottle = _____ L

**40.**     Tim has 64 marbles.
His friend gives him 28 more marbles.
How many marbles does Tim have now?

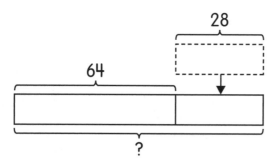

Tim has _____ marbles now.

# Extended Response (5 x 4 points = 20 points)

**Solve.**
**Draw bar models to help you.**

**41.** Ribbon A is 36 centimeters long.
Ribbon B is 39 centimeters longer than Ribbon A.
What is the length of Ribbon B?

The length of Ribbon B is _____ centimeters.

**42.**

How much heavier is Herbert's mother than Herbert?

Herbert's mother is _____ kilograms heavier than Herbert.

**Solve.**
**Show your work.**

**43.**   6 monkeys are in a zoo.
Each monkey has 3 bananas.
How many bananas are there in all?

There are _____ bananas in all.

**44.**   Divide 24 oranges equally among 4 boys.
How many oranges does each boy get?

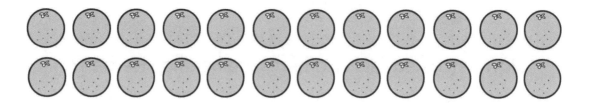

Each boy gets _____ oranges.

**Solve.**
**Draw bar models to help you.**

**45.** Kiri had 325 beads at first.
She uses 148 beads to make a bracelet.
Then she buys 186 more beads.
How many beads does Kiri have now?

Kiri has _____ beads now.

# Answers

Chapter 1

**Lesson 1**
1. 100
2. 500
3. 1,000
4. 614; six hundred fourteen
5. 326; three hundred twenty-six
6. 205; two hundred five
7. three hundred twenty-four
8. five hundred ninety-two
9. seven hundred forty-eight
10. four hundred sixteen
11. two hundred nine
12. 415
13. 898
14. 142
15. 206
16. 1,000
17. 325, 326, 327, <u>328</u>, <u>329</u>, <u>330</u>
18. 432, 433, 434, <u>435</u>, <u>436</u>, <u>437</u>
19. 201, 202, 203, <u>204</u>, <u>205</u>, <u>206</u>
20. 280, 290, <u>300</u>, <u>310</u>, <u>320</u>, 330
21. 315, 325, 335, <u>345</u>, <u>355</u>, <u>365</u>
22. 461, 471, 481, <u>491</u>, <u>501</u>, <u>511</u>
23. 210, 310, 410, <u>510</u>, <u>610</u>, <u>710</u>
24. 306, 406, 506, <u>606</u>, <u>706</u>, <u>806</u>
25. 119, 219, 319, <u>419</u>, <u>519</u>, <u>619</u>

**Lesson 2**
1. 5; 5; 7; 557
2. 8; 1; 5; 815
3. 3; 5; 8; 358
4. 4; 2; 3
5. 5; 3; 0
6. 3; 0; 6
7. a. 4  b. 3  c. 8
8. a. 0  b. 1  c. 7
9. a. 5  b. 2  c. 9
10. 7; 4; 0
11. 6; 3; 1
12. 400; 4; four hundred seventy-five
13. 20; 8; 2; eight hundred twenty-six
14. 9
15. 600
16. 0
17. 60
18. 782
19. 304
20. 536
21. 290

22. 500; 20; 1
23. 200; 60; 0
24. 70
25. 500
26. 7
27. 4

**Lesson 3**
1. 630 is less than 603. ☐
   603 is less than 630. ✔
   603 is greater than 630. ☐
   630 is greater than 603. ✔
2. 832 is less than 823. ☐
   832 is greater than 823. ✔
   823 is less than 832. ✔
   823 is greater than 832. ☐
3. 472 is less than 492. ✔
   431 is less than 389. ☐
   399 is greater than 395. ✔
   745 is greater than 7 hundreds and 5 ones. ✔

4.
5.
6.
7.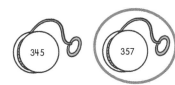

8. greater than
9. less than
10. less than
11. greater than
12. >
13. <
14. >
15. >
16. <
17. >
18. F
19. T
20. F
21. T
22. F
23. T

## Lesson 4

1. 254, 381, 439, 617
2. 431, 413, 314, 134
3. 375, 607, 700, 832
4. 310, 283, 238, 203
5. Answer varies.
   For example,
   379, 397, 739, 793
6. 370
7. 350
8. 79
9. 512; 612
10. 655; 665
11. 310; 710

### Put on Your Thinking Cap!

Thinking skill: Comparing

Strategy: Sort and compare

Solution:

$30 − $20 = $10

 = $10

$18 − $10 = $8

 = $16

$20 − $8 = $12

🍐 + 🍐 + 🍐 = $36

### Chapter 2

## Lesson 1

1. 12
2. 4; 10; 10; 5; 15; 15
3. 13
4. 14
5. 13
6. 14
7. 15
8. 16
9. 18
10. 6
11. 8; 2; 2; 3; 5; 5
12. 3
13. 8
14. 5
15. 5
16. 6
17. 7
18. 9

## Lesson 2

1. 5; 6; 8; 865
2. 868
3. 599
4. 869
5. 789
6. 128 + 311 = 439
   They score 439 points in all.
7. 150 + 110 = 260
   They bake 260 snacks in all.

## Lesson 3

1. 14; 1; 4; 7; 9; 974
2. 691
3. 470
4. 241
5. 832
6. 124 + 136 = 260
   James and Cameron score 260 points in all.
7. 348 + 239 = 587
   587 books are sold during the two day sale.

## Lesson 4

1. 8; 15; 1; 5; 7; 758
2. 516
3. 927
4. 625
5. 969
6. 385 + 74 = 459
   She had 459 eggs at first.
7. 546 + 273 = 819
   Andy has 819 stamps now.

## Lesson 5

1. 247
2. 431
3. 412
4. 575
5. 822
6. 844

MASTER your Math!

7. 248 + 94 = 342
   Philip has 342 stickers.
8. 209 + 85 = 294
   Joshua solves 294 problems in all.

### Put on Your Thinking Cap!

1. Thinking skill: Addition
   Strategy: Guess and check
   Solution:
   529 + 416 = 945
   526 + 419 = 945
   519 + 426 = 945
   516 + 429 = 945
2. Thinking skill: Addition
   Strategy: Guess and check
   Solution:
   146 + 257 = 403 or 156 + 247 = 403
   157 + 246 = 403 or 147 + 256 = 403

### Chapter 3

## Lesson 1

1. 1; 1; 4; 411
2. 514
3. 323
4. 112
5. 152

6. 498 − 254 = 244
   Ling has <u>244</u> beads left.
7. 282 − 110 = 172
   Mr. Garcia drives <u>172</u> miles on Sunday.

## Lesson 2
1. 13; 1; 8; 418; 418
2. 638          3. 229
4. 213          5. 218
6. 394 − 88 = 306
   Jacob has <u>306</u> coins now.
7. 455 − 129 = 326
   <u>326</u> children visit the museum on Thursday.

## Lesson 3
1. 15; 5; 8; 2; 582; 582
2. 185          3. 581
4. 352          5. 177
6. 345 − 172 = 173
   Matthew has <u>173</u> more cards than David.
7. $258 − $182 = $76
   The tea set costs <u>$76</u> less than the dinner set.

## Lesson 4
1. 15; 2; 8; 2; 282; 282
2. 259          3. 347
4. 463          5. 478
6. 430 − 145 = 285
   Lara makes <u>285</u> glasses of orange juice.
7. 245 − 187 = 58
   There are <u>58</u> books left in Emily's library.

## Lesson 5
1. 10; 9; 10; 117
2. 154          3. 124
4. 405          5. 335
6. 452          7. 291
8. 400 − 378 = 22
   He has <u>22</u> more apples than oranges.
9. 800 − 168 = 632
   There are <u>632</u> women at the soccer match.

**Put on Your Thinking Cap!**
1. Thinking skill: Deduction
   Strategy: Guess and check
   Solution:

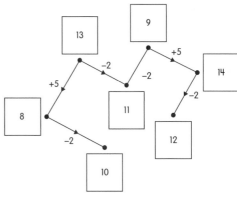

2. Thinking skill: Deduction
   Strategy: Guess and check
   Solution: Add 3 numbers to get 740.
   The digit in the tens place is 4.
   **2<u>4</u>0 + 1<u>8</u>0 + 3<u>2</u>0 = 7<u>4</u>0**

   40 + 80 + 20 = 1<u>4</u>0
   Bank <u>A</u>, Bank <u>B</u>, and Bank <u>D</u> contain 740 coins in all.

**Chapter 4**

## Lesson 1
1.

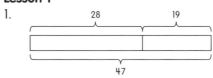

28 + 19 = 47
There are <u>47</u> students in all.

2.

$154 + $78 = $232
Mrs. Marie gives <u>$232</u> in all.

3.

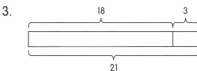

21 − 3 = 18
Mrs. Diaz has <u>18</u> balloons now.

**4.**

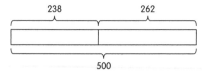

$500 - 238 = 262$

Jaime has <u>262</u> blue beads.

**Lesson 2**

**1.**

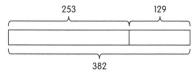

$145 + 37 = 182$

Ella has <u>182</u> marbles in all.

**2.**

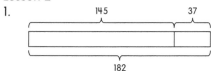

$253 + 129 = 382$

There are <u>382</u> chairs in all.

**3.**

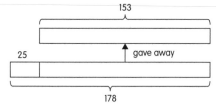

$178 - 25 = 153$

Leena gave her sister <u>153</u> crayons.

**4.**

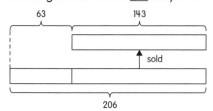

$206 - 143 = 63$

The baker has <u>63</u> muffins left.

**5.**

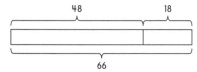

$48 + 18 = 66$

Pedro has <u>66</u> basketball trading cards in all.

**6.**

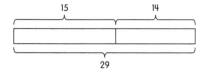

$15 + 14 = 29$

Keisha has <u>29</u> stickers in all.

**7.**

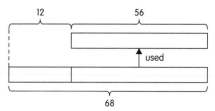

$68 - 56 = 12$

She has <u>12</u> flowers now.

**8.**

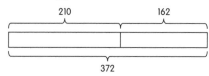

$210 + 162 = 372$

There are <u>372</u> people in the theater now.

**Lesson 3**

**1.**

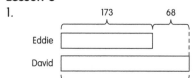

$173 + 68 = 241$

David has <u>241</u> stamps.

**2.**

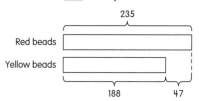

$235 - 47 = 188$

Susie needs <u>188</u> yellow beads.

**3.**

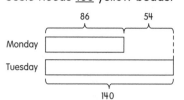

$86 + 54 = 140$

Daniel sells <u>140</u> tickets on Tuesday.

**4.**

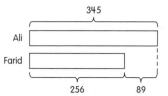

$345 - 89 = 256$

Farid scores <u>256</u> points.

## Lesson 4

1. a.

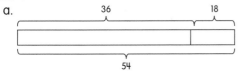

36 + 18 = 54
There were <u>54</u> birds at first.

b.

54 − 9 = 45
There are <u>45</u> birds left.

2. a.

$382 + $235 = $617
Ivan spends $<u>617</u> on clothes.

b.

$617 + $382 = $999
Ivan spends $<u>999</u> in all.

3.

128 + 76 = 204

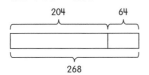

268 − 204 = 64
Peter gave <u>64</u> marbles to Jack.

4.

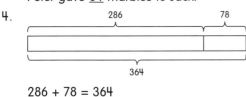

286 + 78 = 364

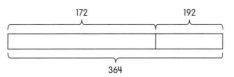

364 − 172 = 192
Joel has <u>192</u> stamps from Spain.

## Put on Your Thinking Cap!

1. Thinking skill: Comparing
   Strategy: Draw a diagram.
   Solution:

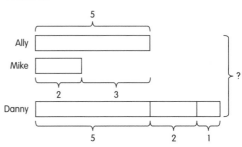

5 + 2 + 1 = 8
Danny has 8 crayons.
5 + 2 + 8 = 15
They have <u>15</u> crayons in all.

2. Thinking skill: Deduction
   Strategy: Simplify the problem
   Solution:

   a. There are 7 more girls than boys.  ✔

   b. There are more boys than girls.  ☐

   c. There are 14 more girls than boys.  ☐

   d. If 5 more boys join the class, there
      will be 2 more girls than boys in
      the class.  ✔

### Chapter 5

## Lesson 1

1. 4 threes = <u>12</u>
   4 × 3 = <u>12</u>
   4 tricycles have <u>12</u> wheels.

2. 10 fives = <u>50</u>
   10 × 5 = <u>50</u>
   There are <u>50</u> stars on 10 cards.

3. 6 + 6 + 6 + 6 + 6 = <u>30</u>
   <u>5</u> × 6 = <u>30</u>

4. Twyla has <u>4</u> groups of apples.
   Each group has <u>8</u> apples.
   There are <u>32</u> apples in all.

5. Louis has <u>3</u> groups of muffins.
   Each group has <u>7</u> muffins.
   There are <u>21</u> muffins in all.

6. $6 \times 7 = \underline{42}$
   There are <u>42</u> beads in all.

7. $\underline{4} \times 7 = \underline{28}$
   There are <u>28</u> apples in all.

**Lesson 2**

1. $12 \div \underline{3} = \underline{4}$
   There are <u>4</u> apples in each group.

2. $20 \div \underline{5} = \underline{4}$
   There are <u>4</u> flowers in each group.

3. $16 \div \underline{4} = \underline{4}$
   There are <u>4</u> groups of 4 crackers.

4. $18 \div \underline{6} = \underline{3}$
   There are <u>3</u> groups of 6 chicks.

5. $15 - 3 - \underline{3} - \underline{3} - \underline{3} - \underline{3} = 0$
   $15 \div 3 = \underline{5}$
   There are <u>5</u> groups.

6. $21 - 7 - \underline{7} - \underline{7} = 0$
   $21 \div 3 = \underline{7}$
   There are <u>3</u> groups of 7 worms.

7. $18 - \underline{9} - \underline{9} = 0$
   $18 \div 9 = \underline{2}$
   There are <u>2</u> groups of 9 strawberries.

8. $14 - \underline{2} - \underline{2} - \underline{2} - \underline{2} - \underline{2} - \underline{2} - \underline{2} = 0$
   $14 \div 2 = \underline{7}$
   There are <u>7</u> groups of 2 avocados.

**Lesson 3**

1. $3 \times 4 = \underline{12}$
   Felix has <u>12</u> goldfish.

2. $4 \times 8 = \underline{32}$
   I have <u>32</u> slices.

3. $\underline{9} \div \underline{3} = \underline{3}$
   Each monkey gets <u>3</u> bananas.

4. $\underline{16} \div \underline{4} = \underline{4}$
   Nathan has <u>4</u> pet rabbits.

**Put on Your Thinking Cap!**

1. Thinking skill: Deduction
   Strategy: Simplify the problem
   Solution: 5 times 8 is 40
   $\qquad 42 - 40 = 2$
   <u>2</u> saplings are left over.

2. Thinking skill: Analyzing parts and whole
   Strategy: Guess and check
   Solution:

 $= 27 - 15 = \underline{12}$

 $= 12 \div 3 = \underline{4}$

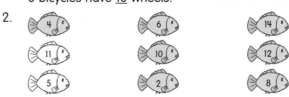 $= 15 \div 3 = \underline{5}$

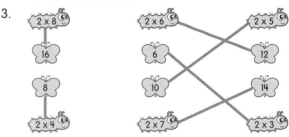 $+ = 4 + 5 = \underline{9}$

$+ = 4 + 4 + 5 + 5 = \underline{18}$

**Chapter 6**

**Lesson 1**

1. $8 \times 2 = \underline{16}$
   8 bicycles have <u>16</u> wheels.

2. 

   2, 4, <u>6</u>, <u>8</u>, <u>10</u>, <u>12</u>, <u>14</u>

3. 

4. 

| Number of birds | 1 | 2 | <u>3</u> | <u>4</u> | 5 | <u>6</u> | <u>7</u> | 8 | <u>9</u> | 10 |
|---|---|---|---|---|---|---|---|---|---|---|
| Number of legs | 2 | 4 | 6 | 8 | <u>10</u> | 12 | 14 | <u>16</u> | 18 | <u>20</u> |

**Lesson 2**

1. $8 \times 2 = 16$
   Mrs. Lee gives <u>16</u> crackers to the children in all.

2. $6 \times 2 = 12$
   There are <u>12</u> wheels in all.

3. $5 \times 2 = \underline{10}$

4. $6 \times 2 = 5 \times 2 + \underline{2}$

5. $2 \times 2 = 1 \times 2 + \underline{1} \times 2$
$= 2 + \underline{2}$
$= \underline{4}$

6. $4 \times 2 = 1 \times 2 + \underline{3} \times 2$
$= 2 + \underline{6}$
$= \underline{8}$

7. $5 \times 2$ is $\underline{2}$ more than $4 \times 2$.

8. $6 \times 2$ is $\underline{6}$ less than $9 \times 2$.

9. $9 \times 2$ is $\underline{4}$ more than $7 \times 2$.

10. $2 \times 2$ is $\underline{12}$ less than $8 \times 2$.

11. $5 \times 2 = \underline{10}$     12. $6 \times 2 = \underline{12}$
$2 \times 5 = \underline{10}$           $2 \times 6 = \underline{12}$

13. $4 \times 2 = \underline{8}$      14. $7 \times 2 = \underline{14}$
$2 \times 4 = \underline{8}$            $2 \times 7 = \underline{14}$

## Lesson 3

1. 5, <u>10</u>, <u>15</u>, <u>20</u>, 25, <u>30</u>

2. 25, <u>30</u>, <u>35</u>, 40, <u>45</u>, 50

3.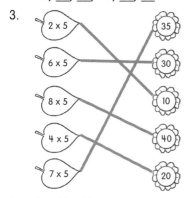

4. $6 \times 5 = \underline{30}$
She bakes <u>30</u> buns in 6 days.

5. $\underline{7} \times \underline{5} = \underline{35}$
Peter gives his friends <u>35</u> marbles in all.

## Lesson 4

1. $7 \times 5 = 35$
There are <u>35</u> stickers in all.

2. $8 \times 5 = 40$
They eat <u>40</u> cherries in all.

3. $3 \times 5 = \underline{15}$      4. $5 \times 5 = \underline{25}$

5. $7 \times 5$ is $\underline{5}$ more than $6 \times 5$.

6. $10 \times 5$ is $\underline{10}$ more than $8 \times 5$.

7. $6 \times 5$ is $\underline{10}$ less than $8 \times 5$.

8. $\underline{2} \times \underline{5} = \underline{10}$; $\underline{5} \times \underline{2} = \underline{10}$

9. $\underline{6} \times \underline{5} = \underline{30}$; $\underline{5} \times \underline{6} = \underline{30}$

10. $\underline{4} \times \underline{2} = \underline{8}$; $\underline{2} \times \underline{4} = \underline{8}$

11. $\underline{4} \times \underline{5} = \underline{20}$; $\underline{5} \times \underline{4} = \underline{20}$

## Lesson 5

1. 10, 20, <u>30</u>, 40, 50, <u>60</u>, 70, 80, 90, <u>100</u>

2. $8 \times 1 = \underline{8}$; $8 \times 10 = \underline{80}$

3. $9 \times 1 = \underline{9}$; $9 \times 10 = \underline{90}$

4. $10 \times 1 = \underline{10}$; $10 \times 10 = \underline{100}$

5. $4 \times 10 = 40$
There are <u>40</u> balloons in all.

6. $3 \times 10 = 30$
Adena has <u>30</u> beads in all.

7. $8 \times 10 = 80$
There are <u>80</u> books in all.

8. $6 \times 10 = 60$
Brooke buys <u>60</u> cards in all.

9.

| Number of boxes | 3 | 6 | 7 | 8 | 10 |
|---|---|---|---|---|---|
| Number of stamps | 30 | <u>60</u> | <u>70</u> | <u>80</u> | <u>100</u> |

10. $3 \times 10 = \underline{30}$; $10 \times 3 = \underline{30}$

## Lesson 6

1.
12 is an <u>even</u> number.

2.
15 is an <u>odd</u> number.

3.
21 is an <u>odd</u> number.

4.
30 is an <u>even</u> number.

5. 9 is an <u>odd</u> number.

6. 23 is an <u>odd number</u>.

7. 34 is an <u>even number</u>.

8. 37 is an <u>odd number</u>.

9. $14 = \underline{7} + \underline{7}$

10. $20 = 10 + \underline{10}$

11. $\underline{28} = 14 + 14$

12. $30 = \underline{15} + \underline{15}$

13. $36 = \underline{18} + \underline{18}$

14. $40 = 20 + \underline{20}$

15. $\underline{48} = 24 + 24$

16. $\underline{50} = 25 + 25$

17. $62 = \underline{31} + \underline{31}$

18. $80 = \underline{40} + 40$

19. $86 = \underline{43} + \underline{43}$

20. $100 = \underline{50} + \underline{50}$

21. 257

22. 258

23. 875

24. 872

25. 103

26. 106

27. 963

28. 960

**Put on Your Thinking Cap!**

1. Thinking skill: Multiplication

   Strategy: Make a systematic list

   Solution: 4 × 5 = 20, 5 – 4 = 1

   The two numbers are <u>4</u> and <u>5</u>.

2. Thinking skill: Identifying Patterns and
   relationships

   Strategy: Make a systematic list

   Solution: 3 × 5 = 15

   5 – 3 = 2

   5 + 3 + 7 = 15

⬭ = 5

◆ = 7

▲ = 3

**Multiple Choice**

1. A
2. A
3. C
4. A
5. B
6. B
7. B
8. C
9. D
10. B

**Short Answer**

11. a. 803

    b. 8 + 6 = <u>14</u>

    13 + 7 = <u>20</u>

12. a. 6; 16

    b. 5; 11

13. 983

14. a. 564; 664

    b. 382; 281

15. 265, 365, 396, 437, 645

16. 406

17. 33

18. a. 305 + 115 = 420 or 420 – 115 = 305

    or 420 – 305 = 115

    b. 227 – 152 = 75 or 152 + 75 = 227

    or 227 – 75 = 152

19. 21 ÷ 3 = <u>7</u>

    Each group will have <u>7</u> fish.

20. 5 × 5 = 25

    25 ÷ 5 = 5

    <u>5</u> marbles are in each bag.

**Extended Response**

21.

|  | 228 | 196 |
|---|---|---|

424

228 + 196 = 424

There are <u>424</u> students in all.

22.

| 237 |  |
|---|---|

155    82

237 – 82 = 155

Jose has <u>155</u> marbles.

23.

27

134

?

134 + 27 = 161

June has <u>161</u> toy animals in all.

24.

103

367

?

367 + 103 = 470

Fabriz needs <u>470</u> green beads for his project.

**25.**

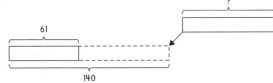

140 − 61 = 79
The farm sold <u>79</u> trees.

**26.**

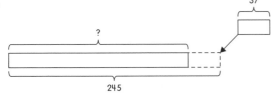

245 − 37 = 208
<u>208</u> people were still at the opera.

**27.**

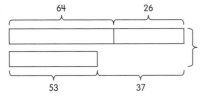

a. 64 + 26 = 90
There are <u>90</u> animals at Dairy Farm A.
b. 90 − 37 = 53
There are <u>53</u> animals at Dairy Farm B.

**28.** a.

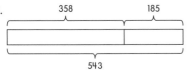

358 + 185 = 543
Lily sold <u>543</u> tickets.

b.

543 + 131 = 674
Lily had <u>674</u> tickets in all.

Chapter 7

**Lesson 1**
1. less
2. more
3. more
4. less

5. Answers vary.
For example,

| Object | Less than 1 meter | More than 1 meter | More than 1 meter but less than 2 meters | More than 2 meters |
|---|---|---|---|---|
| **a.**  a bus | | | | ✔ |
| **b.** a fan | ✔ | | | |
| **c.** a keyboard | ✔ | | | |
| **d.** a sofa | | | ✔ | |

6.

a see-saw

a television set

7.

a bed

a monitor

## Lesson 2

1. a. A
   b. 1
2. a. A
   b. 2
3. a. B
   b. 2
4. a. C; b. A; c. 3; d. 6

## Lesson 3

1. _____ 4 cm _____
2. _____ 6 cm _____
3. 3 cm        4.  6 cm
5. 5 cm        6.  2; 7
7. 1; 10

## Lesson 4

1. Line <u>B</u> is the longest.
   Line <u>A</u> is the shortest.
   Line <u>C</u> is longer than Line A, but shorter than from Line <u>B</u>.
2. Pencil A: 3 cm, Pencil B: 4 cm,
   Pencil C: 6 cm, Pencil D: 9 cm
3. 6
4. 2
5. 9
6. 6
7. 12
8. longer
9. longer
10. shorter

## Lesson 5

1. $24 - 6 = 18$
   The length of the longer piece is <u>18</u> meters.
2. $90 + 121 = 211$
   The total width of the two closets is <u>211</u> centimeters.
3. $10 - 3 = 7$
   Mrs. Feliciano uses <u>7</u> meters of cloth to sew curtains.
4. $30 - 12 = 18$
   $18 - 12 = 6$
   The first piece is <u>6</u> centimeters shorter than the second piece.

5. $139 + 15 = 154$
   Stuart is <u>154</u> centimeters tall.
6. $400 + 129 = 529$
   The length of the model railway track from Town A to Town C is <u>529</u> meters.
7. $500 - 45 = 455$
   $455 - 125 = 330$
   The length of the string of lights that Julius has left is <u>330</u> centimeters.
8. $119 + 21 = 140$
   $140 - 11 = 129$
   Fiona is <u>129</u> centimeters tall.
9. a. $60 + 85 = 145$
      The length of the new toy train is <u>145</u> centimeters.
   b. $60 + 145 = 205$
      The length of both the toy trains is <u>205</u> centimeters in all.

## Put on Your Thinking Cap!

1. Thinking skill: Comparing
   Strategy: Make a list
   Solution:
   1. Stick C is between Stick A and Stick D.
      Possibilities: ACD or DCA
   2. Stick C is longer than Stick A.
      Possibilities: DCA
   3. Stick A is longer than Stick B.
      Possibilities: DCAB
   a. B
   b. D

2. Thinking skill: Spatial visualization
   Strategy: Draw a Diagram
   Solution:

| 10 cm | 10 cm | 10 cm | 10 cm | 10 cm |
|-------|-------|-------|-------|-------|

   She can use five 10-cm building blocks.

| 10 cm | 10 cm | 10 cm | 20 cm |
|-------|-------|-------|-------|

   She can use three 10-cm and one 20-cm building blocks.

| 10 cm | 20 cm | 20 cm |
|-------|-------|-------|

   She can use one 10-cm and two 20-cm building blocks.

3.  Thinking skill: Deduction
    Strategy: Look for patterns
    Solution:

| Bracelet | Colour | Number of beads used |
|---|---|---|
| Bracelet A | Red | 32 |
| Bracelet B | Blue | 35 |
| Bracelet C | Green | 25 |
| Bracelet D | Yellow | 23 |

**Chapter 8**

**Lesson 1**
1. less than
2. more than
3. as heavy as
4. 3
5. 1
6. 2

**Lesson 2**
1. suitcase
2. lamp
3. lamp
4. suitcase
5. 2
6. 10
7. 62
8. 36
9. cake
10. Mr. Clark
11. 8
12. Mr. Clark, Emily, tomatoes, cake

**Lesson 3**
1. 400
2. 250
3. 500
4. 700
5. 250; 160
6. The mass of Box A is <u>600</u> grams.
   The mass of Box B is <u>400</u> grams.
   Box <u>B</u> is lighter than Box <u>A</u>.

**Lesson 4**
1. 300
2. 600
3. papaya; grapes
4. heavier
5. 740
6. 410
7. pineapple; watermelon
8. Package B, Package A, Package D, Package C

**Lesson 5**
1.
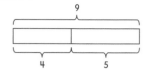
4 + 5 = 9
The total mass of the two cats is <u>9</u> kilograms.

2.
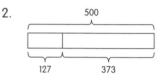
500 − 127 = 373
The mass of the bread that is left is <u>373</u> grams.

3.
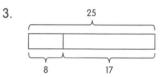
25 − 8 = 17
Stella's mass is <u>17</u> kilograms.

4.
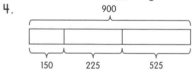
150 + 225 = 375
900 − 375 = 525
The mass of flour Mr. Vasquez has left is <u>525</u> grams.

5.
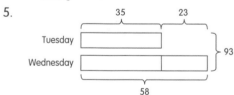
35 + 23 = 58
58 + 35 = 93
He sells <u>93</u> kilograms of potatoes in all.

6.
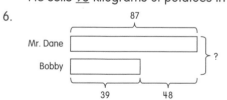
87 − 48 = 39
87 + 39 = 126
The total mass of Bobby and Mr. Dane is <u>126</u> kilograms.

## Put on Your Thinking Cap!

Thinking skill: Spatial visualization

Strategy: Simplify the problem

Solution:
If the robot has a mass equal to 4 longer blocks then its mass also equals double the number of smaller blocks.

3 + 3 = 6

### Chapter 9

## Lesson 1

1.

2.

3.

4.

5. jug
6. bucket
7. B
8. B
9. A
10. Container B, Container C, Container A
11. watering can
12. jug
13. 8
14. 4

## Lesson 2

1. 2 liters; 2 L
2. 5 liters; 5 L
3. 30 liters; 30 L
4. The jug has more than 2 liters of water. ☐

   The pail has more water than the kettle. ☑

   The kettle has more than 2 liters of water. ☐

   The pail has the most amount of water. ☑

5. 2
6. 4
7. 3
8. 6
9. 7
10. 4
11. 1
12. pot, bottle, mug

## Lesson 3

1.

   26 + 18 = 44
   The tank contains 44 liters of water now.

2.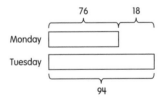

   19 + 28 = 47
   Mrs. Lee made 47 liters of fruit punch at first.

3.

   | Monday |  |
   | Tuesday |  |

   94 − 76 = 18
   18 liters more milk were sold on Tuesday than on Monday.

4.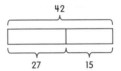

   42 − 27 = 15
   Michael used 15 liters of water.

## Put on Your Thinking Cap!

1. Thinking skill: Comparing

   Strategy: Simplify the problem

   Solution:

   1 bottle → 3 glasses of water

   2 bottles → 6 glasses of water

   2 bottles of water are needed to fill the beaker.

2. Thinking skill: Deduction

   Strategy: Make suppositions

   Solution:

   $4 - 1 = 3$

   Each time she pours a pail into the tank, she pours 3 L of water.

   $15 \div 3 = 5$

   Sue uses 5 pails of water.

3. Thinking skill: Spatial visualization

   Strategy: Make suppositions

   Solution:

   Accept any possible answer.

   For example,

   Fill the 5 L pail with water and pour the water into Container B to fill it up. Pour the remaining 1 L of water into Container A. Fill the 5 L pail with water again and pour the water into Container C to fill it up.

   Pour the remaining 1 L of water into Container A to fill it up.

   The least number of pails of water that she needs is 2.

### Mid-Year Test Prep

#### Multiple Choice

1. D
2. B
3. A
4. C
5. C
6. B
7. B
8. B
9. A
10. D
11. A
12. C
13. A
14. C
15. B
16. A
17. D
18. A
19. C
20. C

#### Short Answer

21. 84, 61, 57, 32
22. a. less
    b. greater
23. a. six hundred forty-eight
    b. three hundred two
24. a. 17
    b. 7
25. a. 604
    b. 251
26. $6 \times 2 = 12$
    There are 12 cars in all.
27. $68 - 20 = 48$
    The length of the face towel is 48 centimeters.
28. 3
29. $4 \times 2 = 8$
    4 bicycles have 8 wheels.
30. $16 \div 2 = 8$
    Each boy gets 8 pencils.
31. 100
32. a. 12, 14, 16, 18, 20, 22
    b. 10, 15, 20, 25, 30, 35
33. 4; 6; 8
34. $114 + 120 = 234$
    The bank is 234 meters from Jim's home.
35. 900
36. 550
37. 440
38. 6; 16
39. 1
40. $64 + 28 = 92$
    Tim has 92 marbles now.

**Extended Response**

41.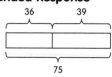

36 + 39 = 75
The length of Ribbon B is <u>75</u> centimeters.

42.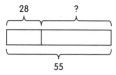

55 − 28 = 27
Herbert's mother is <u>27</u> kilograms heavier than Herbert.

43. 6 × 3 = 18
There are <u>18</u> bananas in all.

44. 24 ÷ 4 = 6
Each boy gets <u>6</u> oranges.

45.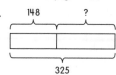

325 − 148 = 177

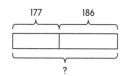

177 + 186 = 363
Kiri has <u>363</u> beads now.